# Crowdmakers

# CROWDMAKERS

A Resource Book of Practical Ideas
For Youth Leaders and Teachers

BOB MOFFETT

Pickering Paperbacks

# Contents

# Foreword

The groups which the materials are aimed at are approximate, and again must be seen to be flexible depending on the personality of the particular group you are dealing with.

Success in Christian ministry is by hard work, so please honour God by using the materials with boldness and enthusiasm, ensuring you are well prepared.

My thanks to Karen Venables and Alice Bennett who have labouriously typed, laughed and mocked as they have prepared the manuscripts as these have travelled through their various stages. My thanks to my wife Jilly, who has given me the inspiration to work on this book. My thanks must also go to all the contributors who have stolen and adapted ideas (like myself) to make this book possible. I will attempt to list those known to me and apologise to those who are not listed but originally thought up the ideas!!

Andrew Brandon
John Buckeridge
Tony Dann
Pete Gilbert
John Hindmarsh
Graham Richards
Philip Vogel, author of the *Youth for Christ Ministry Resource Manual*

This book is dedicated to all those odd-bods who like myself, love communicating the Christian faith to teenagers.

Bob Moffett

# Introduction

*Crowdmakers* is a result of my own desperation to find good material for lessons, epilogues and youth group meetings, that would 'scratch where the young people itched'.

On writing around to my colleagues in *Youth for Christ* I discovered that they had a similar problem. However, after persuading a few of them into giving up their material, I came to realise that much of it was the same, except that it had been adapted to their unique and original style. This book then is a compilation of materials that will be of help in stimulating 'faith'. They all begin where youngsters 'itch' and takes them on to 'discovery'.

I am particularly indebted to Philip Vogel who produced a YFC publication, *Back to School* some many years ago. It was his original inspiration that gave me the energy tb produce this.

My own involvement with teenagers in schools and youth groups has shown that they have a genuine desire to seek the reality of 'faith', but only if it is presented in a way that they can understand. One of the most pertinent comments I have heard on this subject comes from an International Youth for Christ publication: '*We should not be afraid of rejection; if rejection equals failure, then Jesus failed many times; ultimate failure in evangelism is when we don't give folk anything to reject*'.

This book then is designed to help you intelligently inform and challenge young people towards faith. In the last analysis it is *their* decision; therefore it is imperative that you prayerfully present any of the enclosed material, having first adapted it to fit your particular group.

# How to use the material

ENSURE THAT YOU HAVE ALL THE PROPS READY AND WORKING...

1 Prayerfully choose the lesson that is most appropriate to the group.
2 Prepare a lesson outline (similar to the examples given), indicating not only the lesson 'objective' but also what you are hoping to achieve by using it. You should avoid using the book 'on the day' as it will hinder your communication.
3 Ensure that you have all the props ready *and working*.
4 Always limit your session. Finish well before, rather than after, the set time.

THIS WAY!

DO NOT GET SIDE-TRACKED BY RED HERRINGS...

5 Use your lesson material to stimulate questions, comments and reactions.
6 DO NOT:
    – be 'preachy'
    – use clichés
    – be inflexible

9

- give glib answers
- get side-tracked by red-herrings
- attempt to communicate the counsel of God in one session

7 ALWAYS:

- BE SIMPLE (do not err towards being too intellectual)
- LISTEN to the questions so that you actually answer them
- LISTEN to what the group are *not* saying in their questions and comments.
- ASK QUESTIONS that *do not* demand 'Yes' or 'No' answers
- BE TRUTHFUL If you don't know the answer tell them
- BE ONE STEP AHEAD of the group
- KEEP TO YOUR LESSON PLAN unless you feel very confident to move in a different direction
- BE VISUAL

# Part One
# Materials for 11 and 12 year-olds

# 1
# Beauty contest

## Objective

To show that man often judges by external appearances but God sees beyond these and knows exactly what we are like deep inside. People are rejected by others if their appearance is not quite right, eg if they are overweight, spotty, have greasy hair, or are not too attractive; but God made us and so he accepts and loves us as we are.

## Hold a Mr Universe contest

Four lads come out to the front and pretend they are muscle-men, doing all kinds of poses to show off their imaginary biceps. The rest of the group have to vote on who they think should win the title of Mr Universe.

## Hold a fruit beauty contest

Bring an orange, banana, apple and a dirty potato to the group. The group then votes on which is the most attractive fruit. The potato will probably come bottom of the poll as it is the least attractive.

However, continue by saying that even though a banana, apple or an orange look good on the outside, they could be really quite bad on the inside. We are put off by the grimy appearance of the potato, but inside it could be in a better condition than the more attractive fruits.

The above illustrations serve to get people thinking about the way we judge one another. You can then ask for people in the group to give you a list of all that they think is bad in their lives, eg lies, dishonesty, hate, jealousy etc. Read 1 Samuel 16. 1–13 to them. Explain that Samuel was choosing a new king at God's command. However he couldn't find the 'right' person among Jesse's seven sons that were presented to him and eventually David the shepherd lad had to be brought from the fields to meet Samuel and be annointed. Reinforce v. 7.

## Keynote

We can't fool God!

# 2
# Bottling-up the truth

**Objective**

To demonstrate the basic truth about becoming a Christian, and how people make complicated the simplest procedures.

**Basic outline**

Show a bottle and an inflated balloon. Say that you wish to get the balloon into the bottle. Suggest different ways of doing this: burst the balloon, but then it is destroyed and incomplete; smash the bottle, but then the balloon would burst against the jagged glass; or try and force the balloon through the neck of the bottle. Eventually deflate the balloon and insert it into the bottle.

This illustrates that in order for us to become true disciples we must be IN CHRIST. The bottle is Christ, I am the balloon. Apply previous thoughts: then explain that we must deflate, be emptied of sin and self in order to become in Christ.

**Group participation**

You could invite suggestions from them, rather than make the suggestions yourself, adding yours if they do not come up with any.

Ask them what benefit it is to the balloon to be inside the bottle; eg show how it is protected by trying to burst it, stabbing the bottle with a pin!

**Props**

One bottle (do not actually smash a bottle); several balloons, you could burst a balloon and show it loses part of itself, whereas Christ accepts us as we are, completely, faults and all.

# 3
# Fred the Apple

**Objective**

To show the indwelling nature of sin and God's answer to it.

**Basic outline**

A parable about an apple called Fred (or Granny Smith):

Fred has a problem: just above his left ear there is – a maggot hole! A maggot hole where maggot has come *out*, not gone *in*. It gets in by an egg laid in blossom. The apple forms and the egg hatches out. One maggot then eats its way out.

The hole is a *symptom* (give other examples of something wrong: measles, spots, etc.) Find out if your group have symptoms – not maggot holes: anyone not told a lie? Not been selfish? (etc.) These are symptoms of what? *Sin.*

Sin, like a maggot is born *in* us. Look at Fred when he was small – he looked perfect – like you when Mum looked at you – but now . . .

What do you *do* about it? Give Fred a lecture? 'Don't be rotten – turn over a new leaf' (Ha, ha!) It doesn't work.

Put a patch on as a cover up – explain how people cover up. The patch hides but doesn't cure.

Desperate measure: put a black hat on Fred, make him look miserable and send him off to church for harvest festival. This too doesn't work. Explain why going to church is not sufficient to make a person a Christian.

**Application**

Fred just leaves it – he stops bothering about the hole. One day he is picked, sorted into a pile, thinks he is going on holiday but he is told he is going to the rubbish dump while others are going to the storehouse. Fred protests. He's got a better colour and is bigger than the others. Others from his family tree have gone to the storehouse. But the farmer won't let him because of the rot – it would spread to the others.

Jesus spoke of a time when God will sort out people into two places, heaven and hell. Our sin will keep us out of heaven (See Rev. 21. 27) God is *holy* (explain). Fred is very upset.

So what must we do to enable Fred to go in? Take away what is rotten and replace it with something new. Apply John 1. 29, 2 Cor 5. 17 etc. Illustrate what a Christian really is. A Christian is NOT a person who knows he/she is sinful and
a   tries his/her best
b   covers it up
c   just sits in church
A Christian is one who believes that Jesus died to take away his/her sin, and takes Christ into his/her life.

A good deal of imagination can make this lesson pretty lively and interesting.

### Bible verses

*'Nothing evil will be permitted in it – no one immoral or dishonest – but only those whose names are written in the Lamb's book of life.'* (Rev 21. 27)
*'The next day John saw Jesus coming towards him and said "Look! There is the Lamb of God who takes away the world's sin!"* *'* (John 1. 29)
*'When someone becomes a Christian he becomes a brand new person inside. He is not the same anymore. A new life has begun.'* (2 Cor 5.7)

# 4
# Glove illustration

**Objective**

To show that 'man' can only be fully man and realise his full potential when God is involved from within.

**Basic outline**

1 Produce a glove and lay it on a desk so that all can observe. Give the glove a stupid name.
2 Tell the group that this is no ordinary glove but that it has special qualities. It is a glove with a mind of its own that can do all sorts of things.
3 Tell the group that this glove is going to crawl along the desk, take a tremendous leap and punch someone in the face.
4 Talk to the glove telling it what it has got to do. Treat it as a real person. Ask the group to be quiet as the glove must concentrate.
5 When the glove fails to move, coax it again and again by being more annoyed each time it doesn't respond.
6 The glove will never move because by itself it has no life.
7 Put your hand inside the glove and then the glove will move. There is life within it now.

**Application**

Just as the glove is created to function only when a hand is inside it, so we can only function when God puts his life-giving Spirit within us.

**Bible verse**

'*I have come in order that you might have life – life in all its fullness.*' (John 10.10)

# 5
# Your God is too small

**Objective**

This lesson helps to show the vastness of the universe, God's power, and the meaning of the words, *'In the beginning, God created the heavens and earth'*. The lesson concludes by showing that God loves man enough to send his Son to die for us.

**Quiz**

We're going to find out how scientifically minded you are; we're going to have a test (hand out quizzes and pencils)
1  How many stars can be seen by the naked eye (6000 approx)
2  How many planets are there in our solar system? (nine)
(Name them – Mercury, Venus, Earth, Mars, Jupiter, Saturn, Uranus, Neptune and Pluto).
3  What is the speed of light? (186,000 miles per second)
4  What is a light-year? (The distance light travels in one year)
5  What is the distance to the sun? (Approx 93,000,000 miles)
6  What is the distance to the moon? (Approx 240,000 miles)
7  What is the composition of water? (Two hydrogen atoms, to one oxygen atom)
8  What are the three main parts of an atom? (neutron, proton, and electron)
9  What are the three properties of water? (liquid, solid and gas)
10  What is the freezing point on a centrigrade scale? (0°C)

**Scoring**

9-10   Genius
7-8   Good
5-6   Fair
4 or below – start reading!
Review after it has been completed.

18

**Talk-to**

Scientists have made some incredible discoveries about the vastness and smallness of the world. While many of their findings are not proven in the laboratory and are therefore uncertain, the majority of them are very reliable. We base these judgements on the predictability of nature.

If it were possible to drive non-stop at 50 mph around the world (24,000 miles), it would take twenty days. And if light could go around the world it would take about as long as it takes to snap your fingers (one eighth of a second).

The distance to the moon is 240,000 miles. If it were possible to drive there, it would take 200 days. A rocket reaching speeds of 25,000 mph or seven miles per second can make it there in four days. It would take light 1.3 seconds to reach the moon from earth.

Our solar system includes the sun and nine planets, the furthest being Pluto. If man were to fly that distance by rocket, it would require seventeen years. Light, on the other hand, spans the distance in 13.7 days.

The nearest star to us (besides our sun) is Alpha Centari. Averaging speeds that are in excess of our current possibilities (30,000 mph), it would take man 75,000 years to reach the stars. Light would take 4.33 years to reach the closest star.

Within our galaxy (the Milky Way) there are thousands of solar systems just like ours. Our galaxy is tremendously large. It takes light 100,000 years to get from one side of it to the other. And yet in relation to the rest of the universe, our Milky Way is only a pinhead.

The light from the nearest galaxy (Andromeda) that we see today, began its journey to us one and a half years ago. Andromeda is similar in size and shape to the Milky Way galaxy. There are thousands of solar systems within its boundaries. Its size is incredible, but the shocker is this: astronomers estimate that there are one million galaxies like Andromeda and the Milky Way within the cup of the Big Dipper.

The size of the universe cannot be grasped. We, as humans, cannot comprehend such magnitude. Perhaps that's why the Bible gives the simple explanation of: *'In the beginning, God created the heavens and earth'*. That is an astounding statement! I am just beginning to realise what that means. God created everything – from minute atoms to the vastness of space.

Some people look at the universe large and small and say, 'How could a God create all this?' I'm a Christian, and my response is this: 'If your idea of God is that small then he's not worth being called God'. My reaction to creation is among others, awe and admiration for the Creator (no matter what 'method' he used!) A beauty of the scheme of things is that God knows how finite we are, and yet – he cares about us.

There was a man who lived on earth about 2000 years ago. His name was Jesus Christ and he claimed to be God. The Bible says, *'Before anything else existed, there was Christ, with God. He has always been alive and is himself God. He created everything there is – nothing exists that he did not make.'*

(John 1. 1-13) Jesus is God. He created everything that exists.

Of course as a man, Jesus was limited in time; but imagine the God of the universe taking on the form of man because he cares for us so much.

# Part Two
# Materials for 13 and 14 year-olds

# 6
# Be sincere – mean it or not

**Objective**

Sincerity is not enough if the substance of one's belief is wrong.

**Discussion**

Give everyone a sheet of paper and a pencil and ask them to:
1 Write down something they believed in as a child – something that didn't really exist.
2 Write down something or someone about which they were sincerely wrong about in the last month.
3 Write down something that they believe in very deeply right now – a belief you really hope is right.

Collect the papers and read some of the answers. Read answers to number 1, then 2, then 3. After reading, discuss.

Then ask them to evaluate this statement: 'It doesn't matter what you believe in, as long as you're sincere'. Do they agree with that?

**Talk-to**

'Sincere' is an interesting word, isn't it? People write, 'Yours Sincerely' at the end of a letter when they have never even met you, and a lot of people live by the old gag line,

'Be sincere, whether you mean it or not'.

What we have just written down indicates that we have changed our minds about some things we were once very sincere about. Our day-to-day experience seems to indicate that the sincerity of our belief does not determine the rightness of it.

There is a story of a young doctor at one hospital who rushed into the room of one of his patients. The patient was having a heart attack and needed oxygen. The doctor clamped the mask on the man and started turning the valves; but instead of giving the man oxygen, he had given him carbon dioxide. The doctor was sincere but sincerity was not enough.

*'It doesn't matter what you believe as long as you're sincere'* – Do we, or

don't we really believe that? Some people seem to think that this approach makes sense when it comes to their faith in God.

Apparently God is the one exception to the rule. If God designed us, if he started us and is the one we meet at the end, then it would seem fairly important to be right about him. But just 'doing your own thing' as far as God is concerned won't work simply because you're sincere.

What the Bible says about the issue is a whole lot more important than what I have to say. Listen to this statement:

*'For there is one God and one who brings man and God together, the man Christ Jesus, who gave himself to redeem all men.'* (Tim 2.5)

It has been said that it doesn't seem fair that there is only one way to God. 'It's too narrow'; and yet the truth is always narrow. It might not seem fair that the young doctor couldn't use carbon dioxide, but unfortunately oxygen was the only thing that could help. One plus one equals two; and $H_2O$ equals water. Why should we get upset that there is only one way? Thank God there's *at least* one way. Imagine you happen to be lost in a cave and you find a map that directs you to the only entrance and exit. If that exist is narrow and you must get on your knees to crawl out, whereas the rest of the cave is big and roomy, what are you going to do? Wander about the tunnel or get down on your knees and take a chance that the map is right?

**Bible verse**

Jesus himself said, *'I am the way . . . no one can get to the Father except through me'.* (John 14.6)

# 7
# Breakfast time

**Objective**

Belief is important as long as the beliefs are right. Sincerity is not sufficient.

**Props**

Table, chair, radio tuned into Radio one, table cloth, dish, spoon, empty milk bottle, plastic flower, packet of breakfast cereal, packet of polyfilla, packet of dog biscuits and packet of budgie food.

**Basic outline**

Walk in and compose a speech similar to this:
   'I had to get up early this morning to get here on time and didn't have time for any breakfast. But my mum always says to me that breakfast is the most important meal of the day so – if you will just excuse me . . . '
   Spread the table cloth on a table; place a milk bottle on it and insert the plastic flower, arrange dish, spoon and cereal – 'Oh great! Coco Pops! My favourite!' (start eating.)
   Turn on tha radio and after a couple of mouthfuls continue . . . 'Oh! Excuse me – very rude of me – have any of you not had any breakfast?'
   Invite the group to sit at the table with you. From a plastic bag offer some alternatives: polyfilla (to fill those gaps), dog biscuits (good for the bones), or budgie seed (gives you lots of bounce)! After a few moments of confusion conclude . . .
   'Some people say that it doesn't matter what you believe so long as you believe in something! That's about as stupid as saying: it doesn't matter what you eat as long as you eat something!
   You need to eat the right things. It is pointless believing in just anything – you need to believe what is right and true (otherwise at best you are wasting your time – at worst you can do yourself serious harm).

You may well be sincere about what you believe, but it's more important that you are right.'

# 8
# Church

**Objective**

To discover what the church is.

**Props**

Gown, dog-collar, big Bible, cross.

**Basic outline**

Ask the questions:
How many of you don't go to church?
Why?
Announce that you're going to have a church here today!
What will be needed?
Equipment? Furniture? People? Clothes? Building? Use all your props to build a church image.
Again ask questions like:
How should we act/behave?
Is anything missing? How about a person?
Is this really what church is about or does it mean something else?

**Talk-to**

The real 'church' is made up of like-minded people who want to worship God together. Just like some people go to a football match and cheer their team – we call those 'supporters'. Whether the 'supporters' are in the football stadium or travelling in a car they are still 'supporters'. In the same way, committed Christians meeting together to pray, read, sing, laugh etc. are the church. The church, then, is not a *place*, but a *group of people*.

**The church is God's family**

What sort of people do you think make a church?

27

All sorts:- Dustmen, shop assistants, office workers, students, punks, foot-
ballers, factory workers, teachers, rock singers, mums, dads,
sisters, schoolfriends, etc.

What does a church do?

Humans need to worship something or someone: football, pop stars, cars,
etc.

Christians believe God made us this way. Animals survive on their own –
they don't need to worship anything. Therefore if man is more sophisticated
(according to the theory of evolution – survival of the fittest) then he should
be even more capable of surviving on his own, but this is not the case.
Therefore we have the apparent inconsistency that the more intelligent
being needs to worship something. This is more evidence that God's plan
intends that we have a relationship with him, in that he has created this need
in us.

We can worship him on our own, but we lose out.

We can worship him with other Christians (the church)

We can *praise* him with other Christians (the church) for what he is/what
he does/what he has done for us.

Christians come together to *learn* what God wants from *reading the Bible*
together.

We share with each other our experiences of God. He speaks to us
through this.

Christians come together to *remember* the life, death, and the coming
alive again of Jesus for us.

*God's people (the church) are a light* to show others God's love for us and
the truth about Jesus.

They all have to meet somewhere to do most of these things – usually in a
building called a church.

The 'church' can be
– the local church
– the worldwide church (i.e. all believers) in the past, present and future.

**Bible verses**

The Church as – a Holy Temple (Ephesians 2.20, 21)
– a Fellowship (Peter 2.9)
– The Bride of Christ (Ephesians 5.25, 26)
Christ as the Head of the Church (Romans 12.5)

# 9
# Crime and punishment

**Objective**

Due to 'man' failing to keep God's guidelines/laws, God needs to punish us. At the same time God sends Jesus to take the punishment for us.

**Basic outline**

**Law**

Why is it necessary?
    a) Because we are lawless.
    b) Without it there would be total anarchy and chaos.
    c) For our safety and protection.
    d) We need standards to live by.
  Look at examples of everyday rules and regulations showing how they benefit us.

**Punishment**

Why is it necessary?
    a) To deter people from breaking the law.
    b) To correct/reform

Give an example of punishment being necessary for law breakers.

    We are guided from an early age; told what is right and wrong:
    a) Warned against playing with fire.
    b) Warned of the dangers on the road.
    c) Told what is good to eat and drink etc.
Our parents guide us as young children. They know best!

**God's judgement**

God sees that we need guidance or else we would ruin our lives. God has given us basic rules on how to live, eg the Ten Commandments, but we have broken them.

Therefore we suffer the consequences, both emotionally and physically. Eventually God will judge us and punish us. (God by necessity needs to punish because it is an aspect of love).

God recognises that we are unable (as normal human beings) to live as he intends us because of our sinful nature; so in his love he has provided a solution:–

**Bible verses**

Jesus Christ
  a) Takes our punishment (John 3.16)
  b) Makes us children of God (John 1.12)
  c) We can be forgiven for all our past (Romans 3. 23; 6.23)

# 10
# Hobbies

**Objective**

To show a parallel between knowing and experiencing the life-giving power of God.

**Basic outline**

List the hobbies of the group on the board. They provide an interest, prevent boredom, are creative and useful, etc.

Tell a story of a Grandad who has always had a hobby, eg collecting spiders in matchboxes as a boy and many others, possibly using some already on the board, OHP or flip chart. By the time he's ninety-five he's done most things but then realises he's never been water-ski-ing. He gets a book from the library and goes to a water-ski-ing shop and buys:
a) Oil skins and skis, and jumps into the water.
    What happens? – He sinks.
b) He reads a bit further and sees there's a rope he must hold on to.
    He throws one end in the water and then jumps in himself.
    What happens? – He sinks again.
c) He reads further and sees he needs a boat – he attaches the rope to a boat, holds on tight and jumps.
    What happens? – He sinks.
d) Draw from the class that the boat needs 1) An engine
2) A driver
    Use a board or OHP or flip chart to gradually build up the picture.

**Talk-to**

Not by *doing* things do we become Christians, although things like prayer, church worship, Bible reading, etc, follow on from it.

Not by taking one or two verses from the Bible, but by following *all* the instructions (as with water-ski-ing manual), do we grow to know God and his will for us.

Doing all the right things, we still sink – we still fall short of God's standards.

Jesus is the driver, the purpose, direction and meaning of our life (John 14.6).

The Holy Spirit is the engine, the power source (Acts 1.8).

Share personally how Jesus becomes the driver of, and the Holy Spirit gives the power to, your life as a Christian.

NB You will need to explain carefully the Holy Spirit and his role.

# 11
# Power behind the rein

**Objective**

Why do Christians believe that people need to have a relationship with God?

**Props**

Skateboard

**Basic outline**

Bring out a skateboard, place in a prominent position, ie on the table.

No need to ask what this is. It looks good doesn't it? Sit down and watch the skateboard, 30 seconds to 1 minute – as long as the group allows.

Something is wrong! I thought that skateboards were supposed to be exciting things? I paid a lot of money for this as well. What's wrong?

Has anybody got any idea why this skateboard is boring? What's it supposed to do? (Move it along the ground)

Why won't it move? Does it need something? (Pushing/power.)

Pushing it along so that it hits an obstacle.

Is pushing it enough? (No)

What else then? (It needs steering)

Try it. Success!!

**Talk-to**

Do you know, Christians believe that people are like that skateboard! They may seem to be alright on the outside, but inside they are not really doing much at all. In fact, they are dead in their relationship with God.

The skateboard needs power so that it can do and be what it was made to do and be.

If people need power to be Christians, what do you think a Christian is?

Why do we need power to be Christians?

I mentioned 'steering', or guidance too. Can you think of ways or things in our lives that God could guide us through and towards?

For me to provide the power and the guidance that the skateboard needed I had to make contact with it. I had to become part of it.

So it is with God. If we are to know God's power and guidance in our lives, we have to make contact with him. We do this through Jesus Christ, God's Son. We ask that our prayers be granted through his name. Jesus said:

*'I am the way, the truth and the life. No-one goes to the Father except through me.'* (John 14.6)

# 12
# Seeing is believing

**Objective**

To answer the problem of: 'I won't believe what I can't see!' Jesus offers 'real life'.

**Basic outline**

Yuri Gagarin (the first man into Space – 11 April 1961) said, '*I cannot see God; therefore I don't believe in him*'.
Use a transistor radio having first removed the batteries!
Keep the radio hidden.
Ask if anyone does not believe what they can't see.
Show how there are lots of things you can't see that you believe in – ask them to name some, eg electricity, wind, atom, God, noise.
Ask for silence and then ask if they believe there are hundreds of voices – some in foreign languages present in the room. After baffling them (hopefully), slowly bring out the radio. Now do they believe? (Radio waves).

Offer a prize of one pound to anyone who can prove that there are radio waves present – 25p *from* them if they can't. Make sure that there are no other radios present before you make your offer!

If someone does offer, make sure at first you keep your hand on the switch – don't allow them to switch on. When you do allow them and nothing happens (batteries have been removed), suggest you have proved that:

a) radio waves do not exist – all this radio stuff is a big con to get money.
or b) all technicians have dropped dead.
or c) there's something wrong with the set.

Now let them open up the back to see that there are no batteries, at which point you can draw the obvious parallel with man and God:

Man doesn't know God because:
a) Man doesn't want to switch on.
b) There is no life (batteries) – physical life, mental life, spiritual life.
Absence of life means:
a) Communication cannot be achieved
b) Man is incomplete . . . something is missing.

## Talk-to

Jesus came to give LIFE (John 10.10)
  Get connected! (John 5.11–12).

# 13
# Teaching someone to fly

**Objective**

God has given us natural and spiritual laws by which we live. Failure to respect and respond to those laws lead to inevitable consequences.

**Basic outline**

1   Select a victim from the group and proceed to teach him how to fly. Get as much laughter as possible out of the group by getting the victim to make bird noises, flap his arms up and down and jump off a table shouting, 'I am a bird' etc. Eventually after many unsuccessful attempts to fly you can send him back to his seat.
2   Ask the group for reasons why they can't fly.
3   Finally tell the group, if they haven't said it already, that the main reason is the *law of gravity*.
4   Show how one can escape the law of gravity when in a vehicle designed to fly, eg an aeroplane. Draw an aeroplane on a board or OHP and tell the group that the law of gravity is cancelled out by a new law, the law of *aerodynamics*.
    Draw this making the whole thing look funny.
5   Draw the comparison between gravity keeping us down and the fact that we as people are being continually dragged down by a new law, the law of *sin* and *death*.
6   Show how in meeting God a new law cancels out the old and we are set free from sin and death by the law of the spirit of life in Jesus Christ.
    A paraphrase of Romans 7.7–25 may be helpful as long as you feel confident you can put it in a language they will understand.

# 14
# The chair and the pendulum

**Objective**

To demonstrate that our beliefs are basic to our attitudes, actions and accomplishments.

**Props**

A ball or weight on a length of string to act as a pendulum.

**Basic outline**

We are going to learn about a very interesting principle. It is called the principle of the *conservation of energy*. We can demonstrate it with a pendulum. According to the principle a pendulum will never return to a point higher than that from which it was released.

If the pendulum is released from point A it will swing to point B and return to point C, just short of A. Each time it swings back, it will fall slightly short of the point where it started the previous swing, until it eventually comes to rest. There are things acting upon the pendulum, the force of gravity and the friction of air.

The important thing to remember is that when a pendulum is released it will never return to a point *higher* than that from which it was released.

Ask a volunteer to stand at point 'A' of your pendulum set-up. Place the pendulum object against the youngster's head and release it. The pendulum on its return will not hit him or her, but it gives the very definite impression that it will from where the person is standing and hopefully he or she will jump clear.

NB Do not sit a person in a chair for this exercise as at the moment of escape he may jump up towards the pendulum object:

**Discussion**

1  Did . . . . . . really believe the pendulum wouldn't hit him or her? Why do you say that?
2  Why did he/she jump? What made him/her change his/her mind about believing?
3  What beliefs do people talk about but then fail to act upon?
4  Why is believing so easy with the mind and so difficult in action?

**Talk-to**

A famous tightrope walker, after demonstrating his amazing skill on a wire stretched across the Niagara Falls, asked his audience if they believed he could carry a person safely across the wire in a wheelbarrow. Almost in unison the crowd shouted their confidence that he could.

The tightrope walker than asked for a volunteer to sit in the wheelbarrow. In a fraction of a second he faced the quietest crowd of his career. No one even sneezed for fear it might be taken as a sign of willingness to volunteer. The people in that crowd were willing to watch the performer 'try' to take someone across the wire. But they didn't really believe he could or they would have volunteered.

Using this diagram, illustrate the following:

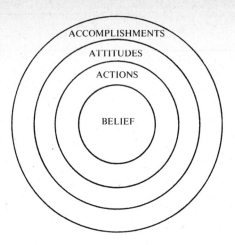

Our actions betray our real beliefs. At the very core of what we arc is what we believe. Permanent change will not take place in our life until what we believe changes. (Volunteer)'s actions told us what he/she actually believed. Actual 'belief' or conviction results in changed 'attitudes' – changed 'attitudes' result in changed 'action' or behaviour and changed 'behaviour' results in changed 'accomplishments'.

Our belief in God then becomes of paramount importance. Failure to sort out what we believe results in a meandering, aimless search for a meaningful, purposeful and 'successful' life.

# 15
# What is a Christian?

**Objective**

To show very simply how God bridged the gap between himself and man through Jesus Christ.

**Basic outline**

Draw the diagram below, without the cross and the descriptions. Explain what sin is, and how it keeps us from God. Ask the group to assist you in describing the nature of 'God' and then the nature of 'man'. Demonstrate how the descriptions show a big difference. Explain to the group why Jesus came and how he bridged the gap (draw the cross with Jesus' name included) Allow comments and questions from the group throughout this session.

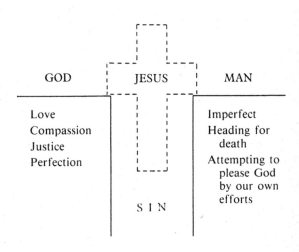

GOD — JESUS — MAN

| GOD | JESUS | MAN |
|-----|-------|-----|
| Love | | Imperfect |
| Compassion | | Heading for |
| Justice | | death |
| Perfection | | Attempting to |
| | | please God |
| | | by our own |
| | SIN | efforts |

# 16
# Russia – doesn't exist

**Objective**

To show that we accept a great deal of information on trust. When it comes to Christianity however, we sometimes accept and assume incorrect information.

**Basic outline**

With all seriousness, stand before your group and offer a lecture/talk entitled, 'Russia doesn't exist'. Ignore any comments or expressions and plough on . . . talking about recent aerial photographs which show that it is just a mass of water – an ocean. Ask if anyone has been there. Invariably no one has been there – assume that this is obviously true since Russia 'doesn't exist'.

When the group start taking the bait you will get questions like these stated below. I suggest you answer them in similar form to the replies offered:

**Q**: But we've got pictures – we see it on the news!
**A**: You *think* you see it on the TV. If they show you snow and people wearing fur hats and they tell you it's Moscow in winter, you believe it? Ha! Just because some of the buildings have onion-shaped gold domes in the background you think it's the centre of Moscow when in fact it could be Brighton Pavilion which looks almost identical.
**Q**: But they (Russians) were in the war!
**A**: That's an easy one! They were Americans, dressed up and speaking a peculiar language just to upset the Germans – who I actually believe do exist because I've been there.
**Q**: But we know of some people who have been there!
**A**: Don't be ridiculous! How can they? I keep telling you it's a mass of sea. Those who have supposedly gone there probably flew to another country. Strange writing is seen everywhere. Guides show you around showing only what they want you to see. Tell them you've been there – you know. They don't even allow you to get near famous monuments like the red wall

around the Kremlin, and why? Because they're just cardboard cut-outs!
Q: But why . . . doesn't (frustration) it exist? You're crackers!
A: American propaganda. With the so-called 'Russian' threat we then side with the Americans – trade with them and support them against other countries. Naturally certain high-minded officials are aware of this and any who are prepared to talk are 'eliminated'.

(If some bright spark shows you an atlas with a map of Russia, just calmly look at the inside cover and say, *As I thought, out of date . . . .'*)
Bluff your way through any other questions or comments. Keep it all very light, but at the same time be very committed to your beliefs. When people are quite 'high' and getting to boiling point, quietly announce that you really do believe that Russia *does* exist.

**Talk-to**

Make a simple point, that very often we accept 'facts' about many other subjects eg geography, science, history etc. just because we are taught to believe them. Often we don't check these so-called 'facts'.

When it comes to Christianity many people reject it without looking at the 'facts'.

Check the evidence, look at it thoroughly, *then* make a decision about Christianity. Before rejecting Christianity then, make sure you can disprove the evidence of Jesus' existence, his death and resurrection, *and* the experience of many millions throughout the last 2,000 years.

You believe in Russia because the evidence is overwhelming. Convince yourself then that the Christian evidence is not true!

# Part Three
# Materials for 15 and 16 year-olds

# 17
# Acceptance:
# relationships

**Objective**

This demonstrates how critical we can be of other people, then contrasts that with Jesus's attitude of love and acceptance of everyone.

**Props**

Sheets of paper, pens or pencils

**Basic outline**

Hand out sheets of paper and ask the group to tear them in fours.

On one piece of paper ask them to write a list of 10 negative things about *one* of the people around them. They must be 10 negative things about the same person, but not limited to appearance – messy hair, hole in jeans, etc. They can also write about personalities. Make them raise their hand when finished. Note the time it takes for most people to find negatives about others.

On a second piece of paper, get them to write 10 positive things about the same people and raise their hand when finished. Note the time, which will probably be longer this time.

**Talk-to**

For most of us it was easy to find faults in others, but when it came to finding their positive side we were a little hard pressed. I must admit there are some people who drive me crazy. They are pests, boisterous or just plain boring.

Jesus ran into some real losers too while he was here, and I'd like for us to read some of these passages and look for clues to his attitudes towards people.

Have a different member of your group read each passage, followed by a group comment on Christ's attitude. Choose four passages out of the following:

The woman having an affair (John 8. 1-9)
The crooked tax man (Luke 19. 1-10)
The prostitute (Luke 7. 36-43)
The ungrateful lepers (Luke 17. 11-19)
(Jesus asked about the nine, but didn't
chase after them or lose his cool)
Little children (Luke 18. 15-17)
The noisy blind men (Matthew 20. 29-34)
Tricky secret agents (Luke 20. 20-26)
Dense disciples (John 14. 1-11)
Jesus' crucifiers (Luke 23. 20-25, 32-34)

Choose three people to read this script to finish:

| | |
|---|---|
| **Jesus:** | May I have a drink of water? |
| **Woman's thoughts:** | What does this Jew want? No Jew is nice to a Samaritan unless he wants something, especially from me! Well, he's not bad looking, I'll see what he wants. |
| **Woman:** | I'm surprised that you, a Jew would ask a despised Samaritan for anything. What do you want? Water? |
| **Jesus:** | If you only knew what a wonderful gift God has for you, and who I am, you would ask me for some living water! |
| **Woman's thoughts:** | This guy's been out in the sun too long! I'll bait him – see if he knows what he's talking about. |
| **Woman:** | But you don't have a rope or a bucket and this is a very deep well! Where would you get this living water? And besides, are you greater than our ancestor Jacob? How can you offer better water than this which he and his sons and cattle enjoyed? |
| **Jesus:** | People soon become thirsty again after drinking this water, but the water I give them becomes a perpetual spring within them, watering them forever with eternal life. |
| **Woman's thoughts:** | If he can really do this I wonder what the water tastes like. Sure would be good not to walk all this way for water everyday. |
| **Woman:** | Please Sir, give me some of that water! Then I'll never be thirsty again and won't have to make this long trip out here every day. |
| **Jesus:** | Go and get your husband. |
| **Woman's thoughts:** | Oh, oh – what am I getting into? |
| **Woman:** | But I'm not married. |
| **Jesus:** | All too true! For you have had five husbands and you |

| | |
|---|---|
| | aren't even married to the man you're living with now. |
| **Woman's thoughts:** | This is scary! I think this guy's a religious freak. If he wants to talk morality, I'll just divert him with this religious question. |
| **Woman:** | Sir, you must be a prophet. But say, tell me, why is it that you Jews insist that Jerusalem is the only place of worship, while we Samaritans claim it is here at Mount Gerazim, where our ancestors worshipped? |
| **Jesus:** | The time is coming, lady, when we will no longer be concerned about whether to worship the Father here or in Jerusalem. For it's not where we worship that counts, but how we worship – is our worship spiritual and real? Do we have the Holy Spirit's help? For God is Spirit and we must have his help to worship as we should. But you Samaritans know so little about him, worshipping blindly, while we Jews know all about him, for salvation comes to the world through the Jews. |
| **Woman's thoughts:** | This man is obviously from God. I wonder if he's the One the Jews talk about. He knows all about me and hasn't condemned me for what I've done. I'm really interested in what else he has to say. |
| **Woman:** | Well, at least I know that the Messiah will come – the one they call Christ – and when he does he will explain everything to us. |
| **Jesus:** | I am the Messiah! |
| **Woman's thoughts:** | Can it really be true? He *must* be who he says he is – the Messiah! I believe him, I've got to tell the people back in the village! |
| **Woman to the audience):** | Come and meet a man who told me everything I ever did! Can this be the Messiah? |

# 18
# After the bomb

**Objective**

To show that a world without God is daunted with problems, and that a relationship with the designer is the only way of seeing the world in some sort of perspective.

**Props**

Paper and pens or pencils

**Basic outline**

A group simulation game. Divide the group into smaller groups of five or six. Give each group paper and pencils. Then tell them: A nuclear war has completely annihilated everyone from the face of the earth – except your group. Only you are left. Your job is to establish rules by which to go on living. There are no other humans left on the planet but you. The only fact that you know for sure is that there is *no* God!

Give them ten to fifteen minutes to work out a new system – and be prepared for some devastating ideas. Keep reminding them that there is no God if they begin suggesting the Ten Commandments or other theistic propositions.

Then reassemble the group and listen to each group leader read out his group's list of rules to everyone.

**Discussion**

1  How did your group decide on the laws? Most will say 'majority rule'.
2  What about those who disagree with the majority? What do you do with them?
3  Is the individual's life sacred if the majority has absolute rule?
4  What about any new children to be born? Or what if you discover a new group of humans later on? Should they obey your laws?

**Talk-to**

It's interesting to hear your rules for a new world. I don't think I'd like to live in a world of special-interest power blocks where the strong rule and the weak must follow or be liquidated.

The idea of getting away from it all and setting up new rules, searching for Utopia, etc., is nothing new, but *something always goes wrong*. For example, if you've read *Mutiny on the Bounty*, you'll remember the men who escaped to Pitcarin Island with their native wives. Even though they had the unique opportunity to set up their own rules and life-styles with no outside pressure, history tells us that because of inner greed and distrust, all except one had met violent deaths within months.

Francis Bacon, the English philosopher of around the sixteenth century said, '*They that deny a God, destroy man's nobility*'. And it seems that if there is no God, we are simply evolutionary animals. Survival becomes the dominant drive. No one is quite sure how or why to set rights and wrongs. The majority? What if the majority favours killing all those who wear spectacles? If there are no absolute moral standards and you can't be sure which group is right, then why not just eat, drink and be merry, and get what you can for yourself?

It is hard to say where it started, but somewhere along the way, Western man began to lose his belief in God as a personal force, as Decider of his fate, as ultimate Judge of his actions. The idea that God created man was called old-fashioned; sin became relative, spiritual belief was regarded as archaic, superstitious and anti-intellectual. Like a son who decides he need not depend upon his father any longer, man set forth to make his own way in the world.

Take away God and you take away the glue that holds man together. All that's left is a pile of pieces. Ignore the Designer and life is just a disconnected series of events going nowhere. Ignore the Father and you wander like an orphan. Ignore the personal creator and you're a meaningless blob of protoplasm. You're without value and so is everyone else.

But give your life to the Designer and you plug into an eternal masterplan for your life. Give your life to the Father, and you find God's love, with no strings attached. Give your life to the personal Creator and you become the personal friend of the God who runs it all.

If you want to start building a new world, that is where Jesus fits in. He came to make God available by giving his life to pay for all our rebellion. The Bible says it so well: '*We are the ones who strayed away like sheep! We, who left God's paths to follow our own. Yet God laid on him the guilt and sins of everyone of us.*' (Isaiah 53. 6)

Jesus is God come looking for me. And that God is the only source of the glue to put me together.

# 19
# Agnostics rule – OK?

**Objective**

To challenge the position of agnostics. To provoke them into thinking about positions they adopt regarding Christianity.

**Basic outline**

Fine out if any are agnostics.

An 'AGNOSTIC' simply means someone without knowledge – somebody who doesn't know, or feels that they want more information before they decide.

There are 3 classes of agnostics:

1 *Insistent* – examined all the facts. His conclusion: I don't know; you don't know, nobody can know.
2 *Indifferent*: – I don't know – but to be honest I don't want to know. Discuss reasons for not wanting to know – prejudice, moral problems, etc.
3 *Enquiring* – I don't know yet, but I want to find out. God does not want us to be ignorant of him and has provided a way of 'knowing'. There is no excuse for ignorance – Acts 17 .30.

**Discussion**

Find out how many are atheists, agnostics, believers.

Discuss what it means to 'know' as distinct from 'knowing about'.

Get the group to discuss qualities essential for a meaningful relationship – trust, openness, reconciliation, etc. Attempt to apply these to man's relationship with God.

**Keynote**

Those agnostics who are sincerley searching for an understanding of God will find it (Matthew 7.7-11).

# 20
# Faith

## Objective

This seeks to aid the group in understanding the nature of faith, exposing misconceptions and applying real faith to our day-by-day Christian commitment.

## Basic outline

Ask the group to picture this situation (be serious). You're sitting in RE, and the teacher writes on the board, '*Everyone needs faith*'. Now think!
1 How do the other members of the class react, verbally and mentally? What comes immediately to their minds? (Discuss)
2 How do you react? (Discuss)
   I think it's obvious that the word 'faith' has many differing meanings in the world today. People often say, 'I take it on faith'; 'I have faith in you', or 'Yes, I have faith, I go to church.'
3 The Bible says that you become a Christian by faith and that faith is the secret of living the Christian life. But what is faith? (Discuss)
4 First, what are some of the misconceptions about faith? These are what tends to come ho someone's mind when 'faith' is mentioned:
   – opposite of reason
   – a leap in the dark
   – when all else fails
   That's what faith *isn't*.

## Talk-to

Faith isn't just limited to Christianity. Our space-exploration is based on faith. Men are sent into space, based completely on the belief that the universe will function today just like it did yesterday. The space scientist has faith in the laws of the universe. How many have ever flown in an airplane? That's faith! You have faith in something you can't control. But what actually makes faith, faith? There are three basic ingredients. Two verses in John (1. 12 and 20.31) give examples of these ingredients.

Put the following diagram on the board, step-by-step explaining as you go.

FAITH **Belief** – in fact supported by evidence

**Trust** – confidence in object of faith

**Action** – personal involvement

The three ingredients are:

1 **Belief** based on examination of the evidence. Your investigation of the evidence leads you to a rational decision to agree with the facts. Suppose that someone says that a certain aiplane is safe. The flight record of the plane (evidence) verifies the information. So you decide to believe the facts (John 20. 31 and John 1.12).

2 **Trust** based on personal confidence in the object of your belief. This act of your will says 'I believe in the facts which say that the plane can carry me, therefore I trust it.' The evidence has proven the object of your faith to be valid; so you exercise personal confidence in it (John 1.12).

3 **Action** that takes personal involvement. You pin all your hopes on something and relax. That would involve boarding the plane and letting it carry you to your destination (John 1.12).

So you see, faith is not anti-intellectual, guesswork, or wishful thinking. It is rooted in fact.

The story is told of a young boy who was trapped on a third-storey ledge by a fire. On the street below stood two men, encouraging him to jump into their arms. One was a burly labourer, the other a much smaller man in a business suit. The boy finally jumped, but – much to everyone's surprise – into the arms of the smaller man. Why? That was his father – he believed and trusted his jad. Dad was the object of his faith, and he acted on it.

The rich young ruler in the New Testament fell at Jesus' feet and called him 'Master'. He had examined Jesus' life and exercised belief in who Jesus was. Secondly, he indicated that he had confidence that Jesus could give him eternal life. He trusted Jesus . . . confident that Jesus could do it for him. But the rich young ruler never became a Christian. Why? Because he didn't act. Jesus said, 'Follow me', and he didn't do it. He had belief and trust but he never took action.

A person becomes a Christian when he has faith in Jesus Christ – the total package.

If you're sure you're a real Christian, what about trusting Jesus with some of the areas of your life you've been hanging on to? Deep down inside the reason we hang on to something is that we don't think we can trust Jesus with it!

# 21
# Freedom of your mind

**Objective**

To help the group realise that our mind controls our actions and that to free our minds means to free us from actions that enslave us.

**Basic outline**

Place an object in the middle of the room (picture, book, ball, etc.). Tell the group that you are going to 'make' them look at the object and think only of the object for one minute. Also tell them that you are going to watch them to make sure that they only think about the one object, nothing else. Start the one minute and wait.

Ask the group to stand up. Then ask them to put their left hand on their right ear, and their other hand on their nose. Then move into a discussion as to whether or not you controlled their actions or whether they did.

The first instruction gets at freedom of thought while the second gets at freedom of actions and control of the mind and in turn, actions.

**Discussion**

a) Were you able to only think of the object for the whole minute?
b) Can anyone force you to think about something against your will?
c) Did you believe me when I said I was going to *make* you think about that?
d) Can anyone force you to believe if you really don't believe?
e) What are some of the ways that a person can give up the control of his mind? Example: brainwashing, habits, drugs, peer group, subtle suggestions, hypnotism, commercials.
f) Which would be worse: to have your body captive and your mind free or your mind captive and your body free?

**Talk-to**

Your mind controls your body. If your mind is controlled, then your whole life is controlled (example: the people we listen to affect our thoughts about life. Sometimes we'll hear a rumour about a person and because we believe it, we begin treating that person differently. That rumour or thought is affecting our actions. If our friends tell us that it's OK to steal and we begin to really believe it, that thought will lead to stealing. Our friends sometimes affect how we believe and think).

Do you know anybody who willingly gives up the control of his thoughts or ideas or his mind?

**Bible verses**

James 3. 13–18.

# 22
# God created the world

**Objective**

To demonstrate that it is logical to believe that the world was created by God.

**Props**

An old watch, not digital.

**Basic outline**

Take the watch apart and put all of the parts in a glass jar. For a more dramatic effect smash it up in front of the group. Give the jar to someone in the group and have him shake it for a long time.

What I want to happen is for the watch to come together so we can tell what time it is. If you shake the jar long enough, you'll be able to see the watch come together. By this time the group will begin to hassle the leader and say it won't happen: 'by shaking a jar it's impossible for a watch to come together – you're crazy', etc. When you begin to get this kind of reaction, play the devil's advocate and begin to challenge their accusations that it's impossible: 'The parts fitted together once, they're bound to fall into place again. You just have to shake it long enough. You probably don't want to keep shaking it because your arm is getting tired.' This naturally leads into discussion.

If it is an intelligent group you could work out the chance of it happening if there were for example 30 pieces; the chance of the watch coming together will be factorial 30 (30x 29x 28x 27x . . . 3x 2x 1)

**Discussion**

a) Why won't the watch ever come together?
b) Why do you think it takes a watchmaker to put a watch together? There are only 10–55 pieces.

## Talk-to

The world is not an accident. You and I are not an accident. Just like it's almost impossible to shake the jar long enough and get a watch, it's also true that man didn't just happen. We were not an accident. Just as it took a watchmaker to put together the watch, so it took the creator, God our Father, to make us. Does that make any sense and why is it important to know this?

The Bible states, '*In the beginning God . . .* ' Nobody knows how or why he was there, he just was. God is. Important: do not get caught up in the question as to where did God come from, just admit you do not know the answer.

It then goes on to say, '*In the beginning God created . . .* ' He was there at the beginning and did the creating.

There are a lot of different views on how things got started but think of it this way. Suppose you had never seen a wristwatch before and then you found one lying on the ground. You would probably wonder how it got there. One idea on how it got there might be that it was an accident, that all the parts happened to collide and the watch was created. Another idea on how it got there might be that someone had made the watch. It took intelligence to put it all together and to make it work.

It's the same choice of answers when it comes to asking how the world was created. Look around you and see how everything is organised. It all fits together. Chrisitans call the great organiser – GOD.

# 23
# Happiness is . . .

**Objective**

To show that the reality of happiness come through having a relationship with Jesus Christ that is real, genuine.

**Props**

Paper and pens or pencils.

**Basic outline**

On slips of paper write 'Happiness is . . . '
   Ask the group to write on the slips of paper what they feel happiness is and give some examples.
eg a warm puppy
going out with John
passing your exams
getting married and having six children, etc.
   What is real happiness?
   Read out loud what it is on the slips of paper, but ensure you keep them anonymous.
   Then read this poem:

> *'Happiness is having parents that love you;*
> *Happiness is being well dressed as anyone in your crowd;*
> *Happiness is having your own room;*
> *Happiness is getting the telephone call you've been*
>      *waiting for;*
> *Happiness is being popular;*
> *Happiness is having parents who don't fight;*
> *Happiness is something I don't have.'*
>                     *Signed:*
>                *Fifteen and unhappy*

**Talk-to**

What is genuine happiness?

Psychologists suggest 3 basic ingredients:

1) *Someone to love* (meaningful love)

I love you *because of* . . . selfish love, performance involved to be acceptable.

I love you *no matter what* – real love eg marriage; wedding service pledges.

2) *Something to do* (purpose in life)

Nothing lasts, even the latest craze won't last: eg teds, mods, rockers, greasers, hippies, skinheads and punks. None of these or other things give a lasting feeling of worth.

3) *Something to hope for* (a future)

Need to win and succeed; a goal; a reason for self-improvement; something to achieve.

Just a dead-end job and family – no real future, eg watch TV; look at magazines.

The Bible says, *'Happy is the man whose God is the Lord.'*

Being a Christian provides a lasting deep satisfaction, and gives us 1), 2) and 3) above.

If you realise you need something lasting and not just a 'trip', accept what Jesus offers – a brand *new* life (Corinthians 5. 17) and a *full* life (John 10. 10).

NB It is important that the group do not get the idea that a Christian is always happy.

# 24
# To live is to die

**Objective**

To carefully consider with the group the subject of death, and depending on time and the response relate the topic to the Christian belief. Be very sensitive.

**Props**

Paper and pens or pencils

**Basic outline**

Give each member of your group a pen and paper and give them the following instructions:

On the page you've just been given, I'd like you to write these things:

1 Your name in the middle of your sheet of paper.
2 Your date of birth a little way above your name on the paper.
3 Now print today's date, just below your name on the paper.
4 Under today's date, write some 'thought' which might characterise your life.
5 Now draw a little line around this information.

Yes, it's a tombstone with an epitaph on it. Kind of sobering. Years ago it was very popular for people to have an epitaph chiselled into their grave marker after they died.

**Discussion**

1 What experience have you had with death of friends, relatives, etc?
2 Are most people afraid to die?
   Why or why not?
3 How do you feel right now, after being confronted with the idea of your own death?
4 What would you do if you had six months to live – and a million pounds?
   As they start to respond, keep probing, but be very careful as this is a

delicate subject that needs sensitivity. You can use this as a basis for further discussion on death as related to the Christian faith.

5 Have you had a close call yourself? What did you think? How did you feel?

6 How would you explain death to a child dying of leukemia?

**Bible verses**

1 Corinthians 15 is a very good passage for talking about death and the Christian.

# 25
# Love

**Objective**

To demonstrate that love demands a response.

**Basic outline**

1 Tell a very funny story about the first time you fell in love (with imagination you can tell a story that will have the group splitting its sides – this really breaks the ice).
2 Talk about love producing a response in the person to which that love is offered. If possible arrange for two couples to act out the following statements:
   A) Statement:   *'I love you. Will you go out with me?*
   Reply:   *'Yes, I love you madly too.'*
   B) Statement:   *'You are the loveliest person I know. I love you.*
   Reply:   *'Shove off you creep! By the way . . . you smell.'*
   The reply always receives an *acceptance* or *rejection* of love.
3 Tell the group that the greatest love is 'When someone will die for the person that they love' (John 15.13). Real love means sacrifice. Maybe tell a simple story of this kind of love.
4 Use this to lead to telling the group that God loves us and he proved it by the laying down of his son's life. God's love for us is real.
5 Finally, God does not force us to love him in return, but gives us a free will to decide our response for ourselves. God doesn't want our love if it is forced from us. He says:
   'I love you; do you love me?'
   We must accept or reject his love.

# 26
# Misconceptions of God

To bring to light areas of misconceptions when it comes to defining and understanding God!

**Talk-to**

Misconceptions:
1 *God is inherited.* He has been inherited from parents, passed down from generation to generation. Our experience with him is strictly environmental. In our minds, God is associated with the past; it is very difficult to see him as being relevant today and interested in our specific problems.

2 *God is a policeman.* He sits behind heavenly billboards waiting to catch people who are having too much fun.

3 *God is a nice old man.* This misconception is related to the first. God is a pleasant elderly man with a long white beard, out of touch with the way things are in our fast-moving, materialistic society – but it feels good to 'worship' him in church. This God is also a little like Father Christmas. That is, if we are really in trouble, he will help us out. Obviously this kind of God is powerless to really understand or help us in our lives.

4 *God is a crutch.* This kind of God is the one to whom we run in time of trouble. He is an 'escape' used to bolster our security. Many people, for example, like to pray, but will not read the Bible. Their motives are disguised under the phrase 'God's will'.

5 *God is a disappointment.* Many of us are not too pleased with the way our bodies have turned out. Other people tend to blame God for death, war, famine, suffering. This concept of God leads many to say, 'I've tried it and it doesn't work'. We are unwilling to trust our lives to One whom we believe has wronged us in the past.

6 *God is Baptist/Church of England/etc.* God often becomes squeezed into the mould of a certain denomination or other code of dogma. (Often when a teen discards a minor point of theology, he discards God too). It becomes difficult to see how God can work in the lives of other Christians who belong to another church or group!

7 *God is a belief.* He – or it! – is an abstract philosophical concept, one of the general 'ideas' we all 'believe in', but not much more than that. God equals truth, or justice, or fate.

8 *God is religious.* He's only interested in spiritual things like Bible-reading or praying, etc. He's fine inside the religious box, but that's about all.

9 *God is a church-goer.* Similar to the above, God lives only in religious meetings. I contact him up there – if I bother to show up – but otherwise, I'm out of his reach.

God, cannot be put in a box! As soon as you try to define God, and put him into some mathematical formula or philosophical essay he breaks out. God is too big for our minds and our finite thinking. To some extent however we need to put God into a box just to enable us to understand who he is. It's like meeting somebody for the first time. We ask questions: 'What is your name?' 'Where do you live?' 'What do you do?' Consciously or subconsciously we put people into boxes to understand them. To put God in a box then leads to misconceptions about him.

God has helped us to understand him by refuting all previous misconceptions by showing us Jesus. Jesus makes this very clear to one of the disciples, Philip. He and the other disciples were trying to understand God: 'Lord show us the Father . . . ' Jesus answers, 'Whoever has seen me, has seen the Father.' (John 14:8–9). To understand Jesus is to understand God.

There are many misconceptions about God. We can discover the truth by discovering Jesus. (John 14:6, 7).

# 27
# The problem of Evil

**Objective**

To show that God is involved in the world and particularly in suffering.

**Props**

Newspaper reports of tragedy; suffering, evil etc.

**Basic outline**

Pass out newspaper cuttings of evil and suffering in the world and discuss these with the group. Ask if God is a God of love, why doesn't he stop all the wars? What about the earthquakes and natural disasters? What about the baby who is stillborn or deformed?

We can't deny there is evil, etc. What are we going to do with it? If we knew everything we'd be God. This question is the biggest stumbling-block to people being able to believe in God, ie the most problematical.

**Talk-to**

*Why did God create man? – Start from God's character.*

1 BECAUSE GOD IS 'LOVE'. Love always *gives*.
Love never forces. The free choice to decide whether to love God and one another, or not, is always implied and stated in the Bible, eg 1 John 4. 11, 12.
If there is no God and therefore no 'love', then the human emotion that we call 'love' is no more than a chemical reaction. Therefore instead of a couple saying to one another, 'I love you', they must say, 'Darling, I'm having a chemical reaction!'
It is therefore *because* of God's love for us and his gift of a free will to us, to choose between good or bad actions, that there is a world of suffering.

Why doesn't God do something about it? DON'T BLAME GOD – God is not 'an aloof stranger' to pain: Jesus identified with us and experienced first-hand the pain and cruelty of suffering on the cross at Calvary.

2 GOD IS A JUST JUDGE: GOD IS FAIR

God gave us moral and physical laws throughout the universe which result in *cause* and *effect*. God would be unjust not to operate by such laws.

If you're an atheist, you can't ask, 'Why do innocents suffer?', because if there's no God, then we're here by chance, which means that there no moral laws or absolutes – no guilt, no innocence. We are then simply at the mercy of 'chance'.

In fact, if you reject God's existence because of the pain and evil in the world, you must assume that the world and its suffering are due either to: 1) chance, or 2) some evil monster in control of it all.

However there is a greater problem still: THE PROBLEM OF GOODNESS (kindness, humanity, love and unselfishness).

The Christian answer is that *God involves himself with* human suffering.

3 MAN'S REBELLION: the riddle of the problem of evil lies in Genesis 3. 1–13. God made man to rule over creation. But when man rebelled against God's commands, the whole of creation fell.

4 JESUS became the supreme example of 'innocent suffering' on the cross, and supreme example of God's involvement with human suffering.

Choose some suitable verses from Isaiah 53 and/or 1 Peter 2.18–25.

*NB Suffering as understood in some other religions:*

1 PANTHEISM: – good and evil are all part of God.

  Therefore the Hindu God is *indifferent* to human suffering.

2 ISLAM: – the sovereign will of God determines all occurrences.

  Therefore God is above, and unrelated to, human suffering.

3 BUDDHISM: – the personal self which feels suffering must be surpassed and denied (denial of reality), in order to achieve a 'higher state' of inner well-being. This denial of the self creates an illusion and is therefore *unrealistic*.

# 28
# Rebellion: change

**Objective**

To show that, firstly, some forms of rebellion can be justified; and secondly to show that the most revolutionary character in history was in fact Jesus.

**Discussion**

Many of us today are uptight about a lot of things. Some of us have become fed-up with the 'status quo' and would like to see some changes made in our society. We won't all agree as to what changes need to be made, nor the methods to bring about those changes. Those who have built today's society, which we often call the 'establishment', may appear to resist almost any change. There are many ways of expressing rebellion and many issues about which it is worth rebelling. But change is not always equated with rebellion, and we don't always need rebellion in order to effect change.

Ask your group the following questions:

1 What are some issues which demand change today?
2 What methods are available to accomplish change in these areas?
3 Does violence ever become acceptable in order to demonstrate dissent? When?
4 When does action become rebellion?
5 We have been discussing the major issues like war, poverty, and morality, but there are issues in our everyday life at home, school, and with our friends, about which we disagree and against which we often rebel. When you were a baby and something went wrong, you would suck your thumb and beat your head on the wall. That probably is less effective for you today, but what are some effective ways you use to make your voice heard? (examples: yelling, sulky silence, slamming the door, stomping out of the room.)
6 Do you feel the need to rebel? Why? Have you tried all the alternatives?

**Talk-to**

We have looked at rebellion. We have seen some of its forms and causes as they relate to you.

We've talked about dissension when it becomes wrong. Some people believe any amount of dissension can be justified while others believe there should be little, if any. Let me tell how one influential man in history dealt with this topic

1 This man was known as a rebel in that throughout his whole life he was always knocking the establishment, and trying to get people to see the *real* problems and values in life.

2 He accused the local religious and political leaders of being two-faced hypocrites, calling them names like 'blind fools'.

3 He once got so angry at a group of so-called 'religious' people who were engaged in what he considered to be a dishonest action that he led a protest right into their temple.

4 Even when he was finally brought up before the law, he still refused to co-operate by not answering questions.

You've probably guessed that this man's name is Jesus Christ – and he probably caused as much revolution as anyone who has ever lived on earth. So, as a person who follows Christ's example, I would be foolish to condemn dissension as *always* wrong.

However, there is one aspect of Christ's rebellion that I feel must be brought out; and that is the fact that Christ's dissension was *not* negative disagreements, but positive solutions to problems. This is where most of us fail in our dissension. Rather than really accomplish something by our dissension, we tend simply to react to circumstances around us.

*For example:*

1 When we always lose our tempers when our parents say something we are reacting against them, not dealing with the issues.

2 When we hear the words 'war', 'authority', and 'establishment', we often react with anger instead of with reason.

Christ overcame this 'reactionism' by stating that there was a positive answer to the problems found in our human existence. This answer was a *changed attitude toward life*, which is a result of knowing God in a personal way.

It has been said that the heart of the world's problems is the problem of the heart. In other words, the needs of the world are a blown-up picture of individual man's inner problems: jealousy, hate, conflict, pride. Jesus' statements about life included changing men from the inside out – and *that* is where revolutions of a positive nature really begin.

# 29
# Standards

**Objective**

To show that man cannot keep his standards.

**Props**

Diagram 1 as illustrated below.

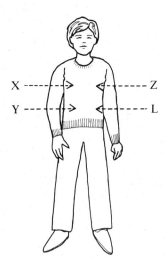

Explain that this is a symbol of a man. *The arrow represents standards –* establish how all men live by standards, although these all vary – give examples.
Establish three basic standards we would all agree on, by asking:

A) Who wants to be murdered? – standard: 'do not kill me'.
B) Who wants things stolen from them? – 'don't steal from me'.
C) Who wants to be lied to and deceived? – 'don't lie to me'.

The problem is not *making standards but keeping* them, eg although the group agree with A) B) and C), find out whether they have lied·to others, stolen from others, eg not paying a bus fare.

## Talk-to

Good is what we want to do; however we find difficulty in doing it – we fall short of our own will. *Man seems to have an inward bias* (add arrows as in diagram (2)).

Certain pressures accentuate the bias:

X) pressures are not our personal fault – broken homes, etc.
Y) pressures are our fault – eg we may give in to pressure from friends, from the media.

Certain factors try to correct the bias:

Z) our conscience – explain the role our conscience plays: it can commend, condemn, but it can't control completely and permanently.
L) Laws – personal laws, eg New Year resolutions, personal standards, etc.
    – social laws, eg threat of punishment (fine, jail)
    – religious laws.
8 But: *all prove insufficient.* Man is worse off than an animal – explain that an animal is controlled by instinct and does not have any other guideline for its behaviour, no conscience. Whereas we do have a conscience. So: what do we do about the 'gap' between the standard we want and the actions we carry out?
    – Cover it up, ie inwardly have standards but not keep them in practice?
    – Lower the standards? (But where does it end – gutter?)
    – Ignore the matter – go through life knowing you are falling short?
    – Deal with the problem within (the Christian answer).

We may try and hide our failures and personal standards from others, but God looks at the inner part of man (cf. 1 Samuel 16.7).

The 'good news' of Jesus is that you can be cleaned up inside and that God's rule in your life will help you keep, 'what we know to be right' (Mark 1.15).

# 30
# Survey on what people look for in a relationship with someone of the opposite sex

### Objective

To show that a relationship with God is not based on what we can offer but on what God is willing to give, and that this affects our relationships and friendships.

### Props

Paper and pens or pencils

### Basic outline

Ask the group to write down what they look for in someone they are going out with or would like to date, ie colour of hair, eyes, what sort of personality, etc.

Give them about five minutes to make their lists and then collect them. From these lists write a selection of about twenty or thirty 'qualities' on the board such as:

a) Blonde
b) Good figure
c) Attractive face
d) Blue eyes
e) Kind
f) Generous
g) Sense of humour
h) Tall
i) Short
j) Sexy

k) 36–24–36 (or 90–60–90!)
l) Fast car
m) Smart clothes
n) Dark
o) Not selfish
p) Not bossy
q) Not big-headed
r) Loving
s) Understanding
t) Lots of money

### Talk-to

Show from this list that we are quite demanding in what we expect from our partners and that often we go into relationships or friendships purely for selfish reasons: *for what we can get out of others*, being far more concerned about how our own ego, image etc. could benefit from associating with this person, than what we could contribute to that person's life.

Make the point that God wants a relationship with us which is not based on what he can get out of us or on how much he can use us, but one which is based on his sacrificial love for us all. He wants to *give to us* rather than just to grab and take from us as others do.

If we want a meaningful relationship with one another, then it can be enhanced by knowing God's love for us. We can then see potential partners through the eyes of a God of love.

# 31
# The facts of life

**Objective**

An opportunity to talk sense about sexual relationships and then to show the facts of life are patented by God and that he has employed the same principles for the creation of spiritual and eternal life.

**Props**

A board with the diagram below.

**Basic outline**

Write 'THE FACTS OF LIFE', with a diagram showing the symbols for male and female one above the other, and the four points, ACT OF LOVE (not lust), CONFINEMENT, BIRTH, LIFE? on the board. Do not react to anything the group may do.

Taking the four points one at a time, speak briefly about each one. Stress that you are simply seeking to talk from a commonsense point of view.

Why LOVE?

Because life's greatest need is love and life comes in bundles called 'babies'. If love is absent to begin with it will be absent when needed and the child will be a deprived child, deprived of its greatest need. It will starve! Use examples of young people who have become twisted psychologically because they have been starved of love.

Swap the letters of the word 'LUST' around to make the word 'SLUT' – do this without comment! It has all the desired effects!

CONFINEMENT AND BIRTH
Talk on the difficulty of these, and emphasise to boys especially that understanding and tolerance are essential.

Why 'LIFE' with a question mark?

Because there are the facts of abortion, miscarriage, stillbirth!

74

## Application

When applying spiritual lessons write 'God' in top circle and 'Man' in bottom circle and quote John 3.16: '*For God so loved the world that he gave his only Son* . . . ' – Why? Point to phrase 'ACT OF LOVE' and indicate cross on lower symbol. Point to 'confinement' and speak of the confining effect of sin – specify sins such as greed, selfishness. Point to 'birth' and mention the context of the verse, implying that faith in Christ results in a new birth. Rub out question mark. Underline 'life'!

' . . . so that whoever believes in him . . . '
' . . . might not perish . . . '
' . . . but have eternal life.'

# 32
# The great escape

**Objective**

To tell the parable of the Prodigal Son and the implications that arise from its meaning.

**Discussion**

Today we're going to talk about runaways. It's amazing how many people have at a young age thought about running away. Like the four-year-old who packed his favourite toys in a bag and headed around the block. As he rounded the block for the fourth time, a policeman asked,
  'Where are you going?'
  The boy replied, 'I'm running away.'
  'But you've gone around the block four times. Why?'
  The boy answered, 'Because I'm not allowed to cross the street.'
  Older kids are not very different from that! They run away and never actually leave home. They just escape through a mental exercise, but never 'cross the street'.
  It gets more serious later on with some teenagers. The Police currently estimate that numerous teenagers are missing from home. Let's fantasise a little:
1  If after school you were to run away, where would you go?
2  What kind of problems do teenagers run away from?
3  Can you solve these problems by running away? How?
4  Is there any alternative to escaping or running away?

**Talk-to**

The only alternative is to *face* the issue. I have yet to know any person who has run away and successfully solved his problems. You can change your circumstances, run away from home, run away from me and everyone who knows you, but at the same time you will pay the consequences.

I once heard about guy who was so fed up with life at home even up to the point that he conned his dad into relinquishing all the money in his trust fund, and then he headed out to live it up.

He did the whole bit – until the funds ran out. Then he was alone, friendless, discouraged and living out of dustbins. He was really at the bottom rung in life. It was in this condition that he decided that he'd rather eat his pride than rubbish, so he headed home to his dad – who, by the way, really loved him – and with forgiveness, love and security, his dad welcomed him home.

You know where I heard that story? From Jesus. It's in the New Testament (Luke 15.11–32). And through that story, I think Jesus was trying to say three things.

*Number One – running away solves nothing.* Jesus said that when the man was really finding it difficult, he 'came to himself'. He realised that he was still the same person with the same hang-ups and problems as he had had back home. Only now he couldn't blame them on his parents or the home atmosphere. There was nobody to take the raps for his selfishness and stubbornness.

*Number Two – a lot of problems originate with running away from God.* Jesus was doing more than just making a comment about family relationships. He intended it as an analogy; the father in the story is obviously God, and the son is you and me. That leads me to –

*Number three – God wants a reunion with us, just as we are.* We don't have to do a lot of dressing up. All we have to do is admit that we can't make it by ourselves, and that we want to be under God's roof. When we say that, God welcomes us, saying *'Fantastic! Come on in. You are welcome.'*

Maybe you'd like to stop running. You'd like to face up to some things, and give God a chance to prove himself to you.

# 33
# There is no freedom
# without restrictions

**Objective**

To show that there is no freedom without restrictions.

**Basic outline**

Ask the following questions.

1 If you knew there were no traffic laws, what would happen?
2 Would you be free to drive?
3 What's the difference in having freedom to drive but not being able to drive anywhere? (No car, no money for petrol, traffic jams etc.)
4 Do restrictions or traffic laws give you more, or less, freedom? (I can freely drive through a green light if the other guy accepts the restrictions of the red light).
5 Can you think of a freedom where there aren't restrictions? Do these restrictions hurt you or help you to be free?

**Talk-to**

There is no freedom given to you that is guaranteed not to have restrictions. You either obey the traffic laws or you eventually lost the freedom of driving (your license is revoked or you're killed in an accident). You either obey society's 'traffic' laws or you eventually lose your freedom.

God also has given you the freedom to obey him or do your own thing. He's willing to let you make the decision and he'll honour the decision. But if you decide to accept God's rule or restrictions, it will give you more freedom.

Example: God tells us to love our enemies. Pretty big restriction isn't it? What happens, though, if we obey? We don't get busted for assault and battering or attempted murder for hating enemies. When you hate your enemies, they tend to hate you back. God's laws place restrictions on us, but in obeying them we find freedom – freedom to find new friends, freedom to stay alive, freedom to walk the streets, freedom to not feel guilty.

There is no freedom where there are no restrictions. The greatest freedom we can find in obeying God's restrictions/laws.

# 34
# What makes life worth it?

**Objective**

To demonstrate that our relationships, belongings, hobbies and interests can only be seen to have any real value and worth if they are seen in relation to the cross of Jesus Christ.

**Basic outline**

Give each person five blank cards or five blank slips of paper. Each person is to write on the cards the five most important things (persons, objects, desires, goals, relationships, abilities, etc.) in his or her life – one on each card. Instruct the group to be serious and specific. After they've finished tell them to hold these cards and imagine that the only meaning in life is in the things on these cards. Next, they should follow your instructions as you slowly give them one at a time:
1 Look at your cards: if one or more is an object like money or clothes or car, etc. IT HAS BEEN STOLEN . . . drop these cards on the floor.
2 Look at the remaining cards: is one or more a relationship with a person of the opposite sex (boyfriend or girlfriend)? That person has just dropped you – walked out of your life . . . drop those cards.
3 Look at the card or cards you have left: does one refer to a talent or special ability you have (music, athletics, etc.)? You've suffered a terrible accident and are no longer able to use that talent . . . drop that card.
4 Now look at the cards that remain: is one or more a relative, (brother, sister, mother, father, spouse?) Something terrible has just happened. They've been killed in an accident . . . drop those cards.
5 Now keep whatever cards or card you have left. Don't pick up any of those you dropped earlier.

**Discussion**

1 What did you have left? Could you live with only that?
2 Which card was the most difficult to throw away? Why?
3 How would you feel if you actually lost what that card represented?

4  What made those cards so important?

**Talk-to**

The cards you held represented you, your identity as a person and gave you
a sense of value as a person. Let's suppose that this circle represents your life
(draw a large circle).

There are many aspects of your life. What are some things you had on
your cards?

List in the circle several items such as:

1  *Objects of value*: clothes, cars, equipment for a sport, etc.
2  *Social relationships*: friends, dates, parents, brother or sister.
3  *Physical abilities*: sports, special skills, music, etc.
4  *Mental abilities*: studies, creative arts, etc.

In addition to those above there could be many more.

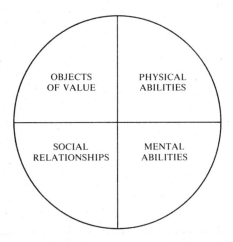

In the centre of the circle I'm glad to put a dot (add dot) to represent the
overriding motivation or purpose for your life, that which makes you
'matter' or gives you a feeling of worth. Most of us have a centre, central
focus, top priority, point of integration or an ultimate goal to our life. We
are worth something. We may not always be able to identify this basis for
self-worth, but it's there. Maybe your reaction to your cards gave you a clue
to what your basis is in terms of self-worth. The things that were most
difficult for you to lose as you dropped the cards may tell you what you
derive your self-worth from.

That is what determines our identity as people; it is the basis for feeling we
are worth something. What are some? (Call for examples here.) Referring

to the diagram, comment that perhaps some of the items around the circle would be in the centre as the basis.

As you can see, some of the bases for self-worth would be good, while others would not. We all want a happy and fulfilled life so it might be wise to know which bases are good, right? Let me suggest some standards for evaluating your basis for self-worth.

1 *Is it lasting?* Can it be taken away? Most objects of value or pursuits of pleasure can be taken away; they are not worthy of your identification with them, as they are destructible, eg 'I am a football player'.

2 *Is it the best expression of yourself?* Many people live with certain values as top priority because they've never thought about what they wish to be. Does it lead to the growth and development of all areas of your life or does it limit you? To see yourself primarily as an athlete or musician may not do justice to other aspects of the real you. You are undoubtedly more than just one type of person.

3 *Does it contribute to your feelings of self-worth?* Sometimes we strive for achievements or possessions that don't really satisfy us. We work for a place in a team, an examination, a college, a job, or a girl or boy only to find that the struggle was more interesting than the achievement. Or the results of the particular basis for self-worth may be just plain undesirable. A person may choose drugs, only to find the alienation of parents and friends may make the experience very lonely. The pursuit of examinations that results in loss of friends, ultra-competitiveness or bad health may not be worth it in the long run.

Some people select a personal achievement, either mental, physical or social as a basis for life; but injury, competition from someone better, loss of ability or personal limitation may place the goal sadly beyond our reach.

Others select feelings of approval or acceptance by an individual or group as a basis for life. A teacher, parent or group may be deciding what you must do to feel valuable and accepted. Sometimes you can't do enough to please; the group or person may change; or they may expect too much and you might spend your life trying to adapt yourself to an impossible ideal. Most of us have seen people bend themselves out of shape trying to be accepted. They become so influenced by those whose approval they seek that they no longer resemble their real selves. They have no identity apart from that which another person or group have given them.

I would like to suggest that comparing your own basis for self-worth with Christ's, you can begin to understand what Christ has to offer.

(Draw a cross in the middle of the circle)

1 *The love of God is everlasting.* Nothing can separate us from God's love (Rom 8.38-39). It is not dependent on personal achievement (doing

81

'religious things') or group acceptance. God accepts us as he finds us. It's called eternal or everlasting love.

2 *God's love promotes the best expression of ourselves as people.* The Bible teaches that the thing to which we devote ourselves makes us its slave (Rom 6. 16) The best commitment would be to someone who loves us for our own sakes, not for what we do for him or her. God wants us to grow in all respects into mature men and women.

3 *God's love contributes to our feeling of self-worth.* The Bible tells us that God loves us before we become 'good', and that one result of his love is the possibility for us of a new relationship with him as his friends. Listen to this: (read Romans 5. 6-11).

And some of the results of the new relationship are love, joy, kindness, goodness, faithfulness, gentleness and self-control (Galations 5.22) toward others and ourselves! God's love teaches us to love and accept ourselves. Then through all aspects of our lives, activities, talents and abilities he is able to reach out to others.

# Part Four
# Materials for 17 and 18 year-olds

# 35
# God/apologetics

**Objective**

To show an intelligent thinking person that God's existence is a strong possibility. This lesson does little more than that as the arguments given below are not conclusive.

**Basic outline**

'GOD, ARE YOU THERE?' The question of God's existence is the most profound question of mankind. Its answer influences a man's values, life-style, and morals. Are there answers to this question, and if so, what are their implications for our personal lives?

Questions to be considered:

1  Should you even try to deal with the question of God's existence?
Yes      No
2  Can anyone really prove scientifically that God exists?
Yes      No
3  Do you think it important to have answers to the questions of God's existence?
Yes      No
Why?
4  On what basis do you argue for or against God's existence? (Why do you think he exists or doesn't exist?)
5  Mention two ways in which your belief or non-belief in God's existence has affected your life.
6  If you believe in God, write a brief description of him.

**Talk-to**

A few arguments in favour of God's existence:

1  *The cosmological argument* – This argument is based upon the fact that all

occurrences are caused. Working our way backwards in time we reach the point where we must admit that there must be an original cause for the beginning of the cosmos or creation. That cause is God.

2 *The teleological argument* – The design of all things shows an intelligent, purposeful, power of mind (being God) behind the universe: things didn't just happen by chance.

3 *The ontological argument* – It has been observed that all men have in their cultures the idea of a deity. Men have the desire to believe that there is something greater than themselves and greater than the universe. The very fact that there are thousands of religions in the world bears witness to this idea. Where did the idea come from? Your parents? Who taught them? If one goes on down the line, it would appear that men have a God-given awareness of him.

4 *The existential argument* – Going beyond the realm of nature we can see evidence of God's existence through his power in the lives of persons living today.

Have any of you been on a Boeing 747? What is the most important thing about a '747'? Is it its size? Or the fact that it can carry hundreds of people? It is its design, its crew, its engines, its wings? No – the most important thing about a '747' is its *purpose*. It would be a waste if it had no purpose. If it took off the ground and never went anywhere except in circles over the airport it would be useless as transportation. Its purpose – transporting people and cargo – is the most important thing about the '747'.

## Summary

*God cannot be proven with the scientific method* because the scientific method of limited to that which can be repeated through experimentation. You can determine the chemistry of water by repeated experiments, but you cannot 'repeat God' or set up a controlled environment in which to study him.

The universe and world we live in are very orderly. Scientists can tell at what time we will have a sunrise/sunset in one hundred years from now. The chance that the world and man were created by accident has been compared with an explosion in a printing factory that would result in the letters landing together so you could print a dictionary with every word in alphabetical order!

We can be confident that there is a God and that he created the world.

# 36
# The identity of Jesus

**Objective**

To show that Jesus was not only all that people described him to be but more – the Son of God.

**Basic outline**

Matthew 16.13-26 *'Who do men say I am?'*
*'Who do YOU say I am?'*

Pass out some paper and ask the group to make a list of who they think Jesus could have been.

We can't ignore Jesus but must face up to his claims honestly and openly. I have a half cousin with the same name as me, but we have a completely different character, personality, etc. There are many 'John Smiths' in the world but all are different, unique people. Others hear the name of Jesus and can conjure up as many ideas as there are people. Mention the ideas the disciples heard from different people as to who Jesus was.

*'Who do YOU say I am?'* Jesus makes the question specific and personal. Our answer can affect our whole future and lifestyle.

**Discussion**

Was he . . .

. . . an outlaw? A Robin Hood figure, legendary, unreal, a good person who had a band of followers and helped the poor?

. . . a Sherlock Holmes, one who fabricated stories for people needing a crutch?

. . . a poet? Parables are a form of poetry, they are stories told to some, with one main thrust to them. Notice the power and authority in his teaching (Matthew 7.29). Other great speakers had a similar power: Churchill, but also Hitler . . . (list a few on board). Jesus lived out what he said – there were no false promises, nor hypocrisy.

. . . a magician? If Jesus was who he claimed to be he would have been capable of performing miracles. What is a miracle? The birth of a child is

miraculous. It's just that we're used to it. 'Familiarity breeds contempt'.
. . . a politician? Explain the Roman occupation to the group. The kind of Messiah the Jews were looking for was a militant and revolutionary figure who would lead them to freedom through war – and the way Jesus actually came was on a donkey, an animal symbolising peace. Jesus was revolutionary in his message of love.

### Talk-to

SON OF GOD:   *'Son of God'* appears 44 times in the New Testament.
SON OF MAN:   *'Son of man'* appears 43 times in the New Testament.

Jesus
God/Man
100%      100%

Pointers to Jesus' divinity:

Only God can forgive sin (which is what Jesus did);
   'Before Abraham was, I was alive.'
   'Seen me, seen the Father.'
   'Have I been with you so long and you still do not know me?' (etc.)

Pointers to Jesus' humanity:

He was hungry, wept, was angry, tired, sad, happy, suffered pain and death.
   C. S. Lewis wrote that Jesus was not just a good man. He was who he claimed to be, or the biggest liar, hypocrite ever.

# 37
# Is there a God?

**Objective**

To demonstrate that there is evidence of God's existence.

**Discussion**

1  Do you believe there is a God? Why, or why not?
2  What is your concept of God – what is he like?
3  What difference does it make to you whether or not God exists?

**Talk-to**

Often someone will come to me and say, 'Prove to me that God exists.' My first response is usually, 'What kind of proof would you accept?' You see, there are many ways of 'proving' things and we must understand how we can prove something like the existence of God.

1  *First of all, we prove things scientifically*, that is, starting from a set of scientific principles and laws we move into the area of proof. But can we prove God's existence in this way?
Is it possible for someone to find the chemical formula for God and then examine the world to see whether or not this formula is present? Of course this is not possible.

2  *Another type of possible proof (somewhat related to the first) is that of sense perception* – we say 'If I can see it with my own eyes, then I will know for sure.' This certainly is convincing in certain realms; however, if any of us saw something we're not sure of, such as a 'flying saucer' or a 'miracle' of any sort, we would find it easier to explain away this type of experience rather than accept it as proof. We are all too familiar with optical illusions and magicians' sleight-of-hand, so that it is easy to become sceptical of this evidence of our senses. Is that a valid proof for the existence of God? It could possibly be, but I'm afraid we would find it much easier to 'explain away' any kind of eyewitness to any miracle.

3 *A third type of possible proof if that of logic and reason.* That is, on the basis of philosophical discussions it is possible to prove the validity of certain assertions such as the existence of God. This proof is helpful in examining the questions of God's existence. Philosophers through the ages have set forth rational reasons for believing in God. These arguments may be summarised as follows:

a) The 'design in the universe' – our universe exhibits a design, this implies a designer.

b) The idea of 'cause and effect' – what is the first and most basic cause of the universe?

c) The argument from 'personality' – is there a more basic reality to a person than just his physical or material being, his mind or individual self? Perhaps there is also a more basic reality to the universe.

d) The moral argument – the evidence of a universal moral sense in mankind points to the probability of a perfect and absolute moral being.

4 *The final type of proof in our world today is that of testimony.* In law courts across the nation the validity of statements, evidence, relationships and occurrences is proved by the use of testimony as a means of proof. This too is very helpful in proving the existence of God. Millions of people have attested to the fact that God exists and that they know him personally. Jesus Christ himself claimed to be this God come down to earth (John 10.30). His companions, the apostles and other disciples, bore witness to this fact in historical records. Testimony, then, tends to prove or verify the existence of God.

# 38
# Moral choices

**Objective**

To *introduce* the concepts of right and wrong as related to relevant moral issues of the day.

**Basic outline**

List some moral issues that cause teenagers problems and ask them to make comments in the respective columns.

Moral issue:
Society says:
My friends say:
My own feeling is:
God through the Bible says (if you know):

**Discussion**

*Discuss* with them some of the issues that have been raised and then move on to the summary below stating the 'advantages' and 'disadvantages' of what the group and you, the leader, feel to be right and wrong.

RIGHT/
WRONG
ADVANTAGES/
DISADVANTAGES
Feel clean inside

Satisfaction, self-respect

No hangovers

Respect from others

Nothing to hide

Pleasure (it feels good)

Less bother from friends

Get away from it all

Experience

Get mocked

Friends turn you off

Missing fun

Feel lonely

Facing the consequences

Guilt

Fear of getting caught

Loss of self-respect

Might hurt other people

# 39
# Situational ethics

**Objective**

This lesson gives us an imaginary case study to help the group see where their values lie. There are no single formulas to apply, only the principle of the worth of the person as a person and the ultimate sovereignty of God over all man's affairs.

**Basic outline**

1  There are two islands in the mddle of the ocean. On one there is a girl  A , and on the other, a boy  B . These two young people are very much in love, but there is no way for them to get together to be married (sharks, etc.) (You could draw an appropriate 'map' if you wished)
2  Also on the island with A is her mother, C. A asks C, 'What should I do?' (explaining the situation). Her mother's reply is:
   'You will have to wait: things will work out.'
3  A is still torn emotionally because of her love for B, and she doesn't know what to do. A then learns that also living on the island is a man, D, and he has a boat. A goes to D to borrow it, but D replies: 'I'll charge a hundred pounds'. But A replies, 'I don't have any money.' D then makes this offer: 'If you make love to me, I will give you the boat.' A, really disturbed and wondering what to do, leaves D.
4  A, after much thought, returns to D and agrees to his proposition.
   A makes love to D to get the boat and see B.
5  A takes the boat and goes to B. They are making their marriage plans and A says: 'I have to be completely honest with you. In order to get this boat to come here, I had to make love to a fellow on the other island.' Upon hearing this B stops, looks at A and says,
   'How could you do such a thing? I can't marry you.'
6  A leave B and returns to her home.

OPTIONAL – Another character may be added to B's island. This fellow is E. He hears about the situation and says to A:

'I don't care what you've done. I'll marry you.'

**Discussion**

1 Rate from best to worst the reactions of the people in the story. On board write down the suggested ratings, such as:
C (best)
A
B
D (worst)
2 Ask the various respondents to defend their ratings. Continue with discussion, asking leading questions, such as, 'What were your presuppositions?' 'What was most important? 'How would you define love?'
3 What was the basic ethic of A? Of B? Who might the characters stand for in society? Only use these terms if you are familiar with them.
Example:
C – parents; perhaps church and others?
B – church
A – 'situational' ethic
D – hedonism
E – utilitarism
You must explain the above terms.

**Talk-to**

It's not easy to resolve a situation like this one. We struggle with matters like trying to define what love is; whether or not motivations determine the rightness or wrongness of an act.

Even when we look at the characters and compare them to groups or philosophies in our society, it's not a clear-cut matter.

I'm not trying to say that all things are relative; but we are dealing with a complex matter and there is no simple way to resolve it.

Let's take a look at 'love'. Some say A did what she did out of love for B. Others say that if A really loved B she wouldn't have done it. According to our society love often appears to be an emotional urge, an attachment or overwhelming feeling towards a person. But one of the oldest books which speaks very pointedly about love, the Bible, describes love more in terms of *responsible action*. Emotion is certainly a part of love but it is not the essense of it. Listen to this:

'Love is very patient and kind, never jealous or envious, never boastful or proud, never haughty or selfish or rude. Love does not demand its way. It is not irritable or touchy. It does not bear grudges and will hardly even notice when others do something wrong. It is never glad about injustice, but rejoices whenever truth wins out. If you love someone, you will be loyal to

94

him no matter what the cost. You will always believe in him, always expect the best of him, and always stand your ground in defending him.' (Corinthians 13. 4-7)

If we do away with responsibility, love easily becomes only the emotional response of our selfishness. And in the midst of an emotionally charged situation we don't find it easy to identify selfishness or plain sexual impulses as such. Our society has led us to believe that there is love.

A second question we must ask is whether motivations in themselves make an act wrong. If your motives are right isn't the act right? If we consent to that reasoning we are saying tghat acts in themselves are neither right nor wrong. They are seen as being neutral.

From a practical point of view, such a position would ultimately destroy society, for who can judge motivation except the one who commits the act? Aside from moral considerations, society must designate some acts as right and others as wrong if only to maintain order.

But here again the Bible clearly says that there *is* right and wrong and that it exists apart from one's motivations. The central issue, though, is not the only necessity to adhere to a moral code that we might find somewhere in the pages of the Bible or another religious book. In fact, one of the writers of the New Testament says that the Ten Commandments never really made anyone good. They pointed out just how bad man was.

The basic issue is how we regard one another and ourselves. Are we only objects or are we people? D used A, but A used D too. Now D's aim may not sound as honourable as A's but they both regarded each other as objects.

God's plan for man is that he realises his full personhood. Jesus said, *I have come that you might have a more abundant life.'* (John 10.10) If this is true, and Jesus went to the extreme to prove his seriousness (he gave his life to overcome Satan's dehumanising power), then God's instructions to us regarding right and wrong are really for our own benefit.

I can't say that if A had waited all would have turned out well. We don't know that part of the story. But we do know that she did violate God's principles.

Of course D wasn't much better. And what about B, C and E? They raise more questions – such as forgiveness, and relationships between the generations. *But the issue is right and wrong.*

You can resolve this issue in your life before you are ever faced with the decision and certainly before you find yourself having to patch up a mistake. *Now* is the time to determine what your values are. Are people, people? Or are they things? Not all situations will be easy to decide, but it doesn't hurt to start preparing now.

# 40
# Truth: resurrection

**Objective**

To show that the resurrection story can be reasonably accepted.

**Basic outline**

Some people today have serious doubts about the existence of God. Others doubt whether the whole idea of Christianity is true, and if it is, they wonder if it makes any difference. Most ok us no matter how much we believe, or how long we've believed it, have doubts. If Christianity is true, it should stand the test.

Tests of truth:

1 Logical consistency – does it make sense?
2 Historical verification – do the historical records show a consistency with regard to important details?
3 Existential relevance – can Christianity make any difference to an individual or a group of people?

Christianity CAN stand these tests, because:

I *It answers major questions; it makes sense:*
  A) *Purpose in life* – It gives a meaning to birth, death and destiny. Alternative – 'eat, drink, be merry etc . . . for tomorrow we die!'
  B) *Psychological problems* – Totally committed Christians have a source of strength to meet these.
  C) *Suffering* (war etc.) – a result of man's self centredness. For the Christian, a purpose in suffering can be found.

II *It is verifiable historically:*

  A) 300 Bible prophecies fulfilled.
  B) Bible – written over a span of 1,500 years, with 40 authors, three

continents, 66 books but is one compatible story.

C) Non-Christian sources – Tacitus, Suetonisus, Lucien, Josephus – verify Christ's life, death and resurrection.

This raised the key question of Jesus' resurrection. Many who have questioned the validity of Christianity and even the existence of Jesus have said that it all hangs on one event, the resurrection. If the resurrection truly happened, then all the teachings of Christ can be believed, including his being the Son of God. In summary, Christ was either a liar, a lunatic, or Lord.

Implications:

– Jesus claimed to be God: if true, then he is God.
– If false and he knew it, then he is an impostor.
– If false and he didn't know it, then he's insane.

Facts about the Resurrection:

1 *Stolen body theory*

In a crime one needs a culprit, and the culprit needs a motive. Therefore the questions are *who*, and *why*?

a) *Jews?*

No – they attacked Jesus. The Pharisees wanted him and paid 30 pieces of silver to get him alive. The Jews could have produced the body at a later date to denounce the resurrection ideas.

b) *Romans?*

No – they were the last to want Christ alive . . . Roman seal and guards . . . If the guard was found to be sleeping or the seal had been tampered with – the punishment was death! They would have produced the body because Christianity threatened their empire – allegiance to a God other than Caesar. Later on Christians were heavily persecuted for this very reason.

c) *Disciples?*

Hardly – would they have stolen the body, hidden it, and then gone through terrible persecutions and died for a lie? One of them would have given in, but none did. Remember their character – they all left Christ when the trouble started in the garden. Only a living Christ could have inspired this courage.

d) *Grave robbers?*

No – rock sealed the grave.

Roman seal and guards.

2 *Swoon theory*

Jesus passed out on the cross, never died, but revived in the coolness of the tomb.

No – The Roman soldiers made sure he was dead when they pierced his side. Furthermore, he was wrapped up like a mummy. It was recorded in the Bible that the grave clothes were still in the grave when witnesses went in.

3 *Hallucination theory*
   a) Hallucinations don't appear to hundreds at once, or even to several
      people.
   b) They don't last long.
   c) You can't touch them.

4 *Wrong tomb theory*
   a) It was hewn out of solid rock.
   b) If it was wrong, all the Romans had to do was to produce the body.
   c) Peter would have made sure.
   d) Thousands of Christians would have found the facts out before being
      thrown to the lions.

**Talk-to**

Christianity is both consistent and verifiable. That leaves us with one test:
does it make any difference?

III *Christianity is relevant today*

   A) Other religions of the world are impersonal. They emphasise ethics
      or a philosophy. Christians talked about a *person*, Christ.
   B) Jesus promised a better quality of life (John 10. 10).
      1 If what Christ said was true, we should try to make him known to
        everyone.
      2 If what Christ said was false, we should do everything we can to get
        rid of this cruel hoax and join the humanists because life is short so
        let's not waste our time.
   C) The Apostle Paul wrote about a new life (2 Corinthians 5.17) and
      transformation (Romans 12.1).
The early Christians bet their lives on the fact Christ was alive – the
non-Christians were betting their lives on one of the other theories.

WHICH ARE YOU GOING TO STAKE YOUR LIFE ON?

# 41
# 'What is Truth?' . . . said Pilate

**Objective**

To explain words like 'objective', 'absolute' and 'relative'. Useful as a 'starter', preparing the ground for a discussion of 'Truth'.

**Basic outline**

1 OBJECTIVE – the truth exists regardless of one's perception of it.
2 SUBJECTIVE – the truth as perceived. This may differ from what it actually is. For instance at sunset, the sun is actually below the horizon even though we still see it. Refraction makes it appear above the horizon.
3 ABSOLUTE – the truth is unchangeable. This is what most people normally think of when they think of truth.
4 RELATIVE – the truth depends on certain presuppositions.

Examples

1 It's warm outside (30° C)
   (O-R) An objective statement depending on what one considers to be warm.
2 The temperature is 30° C
   (O-A) An objective statement of fact.
3 It feels like 30° C
   (S-A) A judgement that states truth like a fact.
4 It feels warm outside (30° C)
   (S-R) An opinion that depends on what one considers warm.

# PART FIVE
## Poetry and Stories

# 42
# Buster Sam and the hanging of Brother Jim

I ain't a man of words; my guns do my talkin' for me, but there comes a time in a man's life when forty-five slugs ain't no substitute for a few chosen words. I gotta be honest! It's been a blood-stained sun that's shone on my dust trails across the prairies an' cattle towns of the west. I've done my fair share of killin'; I've seen many die at the wrong end of a smokin' gun; I've left women widows and children orphans; both my hands stained with other men's blood, bad hombres who raped women, rustled cattle, held up stage coaches and left better men than themselves bleedin' in the gutter with a coward's bullet in the back, but Brother Jim was just about the last person I wanted to plug.

Buster Sam was the dirtiest hired killer I'd ever exchanged bullets with (his conscience was so full of bullet holes that it didn't work natural' anymore). His guns always spoke from behind and very few had time to reply. I was one of the lucky ones; I managed to ease a couple of slugs into his ugly carcass.

Yeah, I remember! It was autumn. There'd been a lot of killin' and a number of robberies. A few of the border towns were deserted. They were no more than shot-out tombs for the dead, ghost towns full of the echoes of Winchesters and Colts; blood stained the walls an' streets like graffiti and told the message, *'The Gun Rules – Okay!'* When there's no 'Order', the law becomes the fastest gun an' the sharpest eye. I've lived long enough to know that there ain't no justice in this sort of rule.

Well, let me go on with my story. The good citizens of Dodge City (Kansas), the bad excluded, had asked me to wear the Sheriff's Badge. I ain't no coward, but once you have the badge, you become the target for every trigger happy cowboy. They'd killed the last seven sheriffs and none of them had lasted for more than a couple of weeks. But let me tell you now, I weren't gonna bite the dust an' wear a wooden coffin – No, pard. I was not! If you're a sheriff, you've got two alternatives: you either die young or become famous – I became famous! I was known in a thousand towns as the 'widow maker'. I was the real, original undertakers' dream!

It was during my term of office as the good citizens' 'hired gun' that I first came into contact with Buster Sam. He drew a gun on me in the Slate Street Saloon. I saw his reflection in the mirror and dived clear; the bullet hit a barmaid between the eyes; her blood tore the makeup from her face. As I went down to avoid the bullet, I pulled my guns on him and fired as I fell. I saw him stagger backwards with his big hands tryin' to plug a hole in his stomach, but by the time I'd gotten myself up from the floor, he'd climbed on his horse and hit out of town.

After Buster Sam had got a few innocent people in the back, robbed the Dodge City Bank and generally made a nuisance of himself, I started to get round to thinkin' that my bullet should have hit him six inches higher up. The good citizens who wanted the protection of a 'hired gun' began to get a little fidgety an' make all sorts of suggestions like I was gettin' nervous of meetin' Buster Sam, or had I strained my trigger finger while playin' my banjo. There was talk in the town of contractin' another fightin' man from Texas and pinnin' my badge on his lapel. I heard a lot about this hombre and a buddy of mine an I wasn't too impressed with his chance of livin'.

It appears that he was very good at killin' men without a gun and never missed a shot from behind, but when you saw his face along the sights of a gun, he had a yellow complexion – any man with a fast trigger finger could see that.

I thought that maybe Buster Sam would hit the trail out of town, but he played God and sent a rain of blood down on the city an' I had no choice but to jump on the back of my horse and hunt him like a wild dog. Buster Sam didn't have much brain in that head of his. He left a trail that a blind Indian could've followed. After about four hours hard ridin' I came across his camp. I was just about to climb from my horse when a shot rang out and my horse died under me. I thanked Buster Sam for savin' me the trouble of climbin' out of my saddle! I noticed that where the shot came from and determined to climb round behind him and slip my handcuffs over his wrists. I'd left my hat on a shelf of rock as a decoy and Buster Sam had been using it for target practice during my absence. I had a hunch that I wouldn't be wearing it again – it might not be rain-proof! I climbed up behind him without bein' detected. He was making so much noise shootin' at my hat that he could've been surprised by a cavalry division. I could see the brim of his sombrero and the silver barrel of his rifle. To divert his attention, I threw a stone. He leapt up and covered the area where the stone had landed with his Winchester. This just gave me the opportunity that I needed to close in behind him for the kill. 'Hi Buster!' I said, 'Doin' anythin' special?' He swung round with his rifle levelled. His face was as grey as a dust bowl. Before he had an opportunity to aim properly I'd taken his gun from his nerveless fingers with a bullet through the shoulder. He came easy. I rode on his horse back to Dodge City and he stumbled behind on the end of a rope. In less than no time he was scowlin' at me from behind the bars of the jail house. The wild dog had been tamed!

The trial was finished with quick' an' Buster Sam knew he was gonna be finished with quicker. We'd arranged a little 'necktie party', the judge, jury an' a few friendly citizens, just for his benefit. He was gonna be the centre of attention. 'Case you don't understan' my way of talkin', we'd decided to hang him. All the good an' friendly citizens turned out to watch the spectacle. They always had a holiday every time someone got hung! Buster Sam had his arms tied behind his back and the loop of the noose was caressing his neck friendly like – that hemp rope would give him his last embrace! The hangman was just about to kick away the supports and send Buster Sam swingin, to a nasty end when a big voice disturbed the proceedings.

'Hold on a minute!'

Every head turned and who should ride into the crowd but Brother Jim. He was everybody's Brother but nobody's fool. He pushed his way through the crowd and jumped onto the hangin' platform. He handed his gun to the judge, gave an envelope to Buster Sam, and took the noose from his neck and placed it round his own. It was common knowledge in Dodge City that Buster Sam had raped and shot Brother Jim's sister. There had been a lot of hate an' even bullets passin' between both, an' that is what surprised us all. Brother Jim was prepared to die in the place of Buster Sam – no one could persuade him differently. The Judge gave the signal, the hangman kicked away the supports an' Brother Jim was danglin' like a spider on the end of the rope. Buster Sam was lookin' with a beauiful expression on his face. He said afterwards that it was the first time that anyone had done anything good an' kind to him. Brother Jim's envelope contained his will, an' in that will he gave all his property an' money to Buster Sam. Buster Sam hung up his Colts shortly afterwards and opened a store. He's become a good citizen with a

A preacher man rode into Dodge City shortly after the hangin' of Brother Jim. He told us how God had sent his Son into the world to die for all of us. He said that we were all guilty and deserved to die because we had broken God's Law. His eyes spat fire like my guns and his words stung like bullets. He went on to say that Jesus, the Son of God, died like Brother Jim. He took our place and bore our guilt just as Brother Jim had done for Buster Sam. I'm thinkin' of hangin' my guns too!

# 43
# Drama sketches

### 1 Umbrella Sketch

Musician singing with guitar *'I'm singing in the rain'* or *'Raindrops keep falling on my head'*. Man enters, finds rain, puts up umbrella, starts to sing along with musician, but out of tune. Musician stops, and insists that if he joins in he must put down his umbrella. Man puts down umbrella and joins in, and they both get wet. Points out that we all have umbrellas sheltering us from life, need to close it even if it is umcomfortable at times.

### 2 Packet from God

God gives a beautiful parcel to postman, who cycles to front and delivers parcel to man. Man examines parcel, looks pleased, rubs his hands, puts it down on one side, and brings out tatty beaten-up package, which he gives to postman to be delivered to God. God asks, 'Aren't you going to open the parcel?' Man scratches head and walks off. In summing up, point out that what we give to God is very little. However what God gives to us is more than we could ever imagine.

### 3 Door Sketch

Man reading paper behind door, ignores the knocking at door from man with telegram with important news. Makes various excuses for ignoring knocking; postman goes and man has heart attack and dies. After a while, he stands up, goes to door, knocks for it to be opened, pleads that he has been a good man etc . . . but nothing happens. This sketch virtually needs no summing up.

### 4 Crawling and walking

Two or three people crawling on stage demonstrating their powers at crawling and the things they can do at that level. A man comes in walking, and tries to persuade them to walk. They steadfastly refuse and mock him, except one who manages to stand on his feet and, assisted by the person walking, is led off-stage.

# 44
# God and the Prime Minister

'Who are you?' said the Prime Minister.

'I am God', replied the stranger.

'Ha, ha, I don't believe it. Show me a miracle.'

And God showed the Prime Minister the miracle of birth.

'That is nothing,' said the Prime Minister, 'my scientists are creating life in test tubes and have nearly solved the secret of heredity. Artificial insemination is more certain than your lackadaisical methods, and by cross-breeding we are producing fish and mammals to our own design. Show me a proper miracle.'

And God caused the sky to darken and the hailstones came pouring down.

The Prime Minister picked up his telephone. 'Ugh, send up a "Met" plane and sprinkle the clouds with silver chloride crystals.'

And the met plane went up and sprinkled the clouds that darkened the sky and the hailstones topped pouring down and the sun shone brightly.

'Show me another,' and God caused a plague of frogs to descend upon the land.

The Prime Minister picked up his telephone. 'Ugh, get me the Ministry of Agriculture and Fisheries and instruct them to procure a frog killer as myxomatosis killed rabbits.'

And soon the land was free from frogs and the people gave thanks to the Prime Minister and erected laboratories in his name.

'Show me another,' and God caused the sea to divide.

The Prime Minister picked up his telephone to the Polaris submarine. 'Ugh, log a few ICBM's into the Antarctic, will you, old chap?'

And soon the ice cap melted and the sea came rushing back.

'I will kill all the first born,' said God.

'Paltry tricks,' said the Prime Minister 'watch this', and he pressed the button on his desk and missiles flew to their pre-ordained destination, and 'H' bombs split the world asunder and radio-activity killed every mortal thing.

'I can raise the dead,' said God.

'Please,' said the Prime Minister in his cardboard coffin, 'let me live again.'

'Why? Who are you?' said God closing the lid.

# 45
# Humpty-Dumpty

### The creation of Humtpy-Dumpty

Humpty-Dumpty was the first egg to ever have 'eggsisted'. He was placed on a high wall by a wise and noble King and commanded never to leave his position of vantage. 'If you attempt to climb from the wall, Humpty-Dumpty,' said the wise King, 'you'll be smashed into a million pieces.'

There was, in this great and rich kingdom, a wicked and cunning bandit who went by the name of Mr Fox. He learnt of Humpty-Dumpty and the King's command concerning him and decided that he would pay the handsome egg a personal visit. His thoughts were dark and treacherous.

*Mr Fox:* 'Good morning!'

*Humpty Dumpty:* 'Good morning my fine sir! It's so nice to have a visitor when you're here all alone.'

*Mr F:* 'Long have I waited to see such a handsome egg. Your shell shines like ivory and your yolk is as the gold in the mountains. If only I was younger – if only I was younger, I'd . . . '

*H-D:* 'If you were only younger, what would you do?'

*Mr F:* 'I'd ask for your hand in marriage. Tell me, fine egg, why do you sit on the wall all day long and watch the sun sail from east to west like a royal barge? Have you never wished to roll across the meadow in spring or glide with the swans along the gurgling, chattering river towards the sea? Have you never wished to sail with the mariners on a ship with four masts to different places? Is there no longing in your heart for the market place in the city or the maypole dance on the village green?'

*H-D:* 'I'm afraid, kind sir, that I'm not able to climb from the wall. The King, may he live forever, has commanded me never to climb from the security of the wall. If I do so, I'll be ruined.'

*Mr F:* 'Ruined! Ruined, did you say? Rubbish! I thought that you were an intelligent egg, a discerning egg, but it appears that you're a gullible and stupid egg. Has it never occurred to you that the King is frightened of rivalry; he knows that if you were to climb down from the wall, all men would follow you; his throne would become your seat, his palace would be your residence and his kingdom would become yours forever. You are indeed a stupid egg!'

*H-D*: 'Oh! I never thought of it like that!'

*Mr F:* 'Look Humpty! Look! In the distance you can see the ocean curling across a stretch of gold, a lake hidden in the hollow of the hills, and beyond, the mountains. In the foreground, look, you can see the villages and the winding roads that wander lazily towards the city. Look! the morning sun has kissed the spires of the castle and she smiles in welcome. That place is yours – yes, yours, Humpty-Dumpty, if only you dare climb from the wall.'

*H-D*: (Humpty climbs to the edge of the wall) 'Farewell!' (Humpty throws himself from the wall. As he falls his screams are drowned by the sinister laughter of Mr Fox.)

*Mr F:* 'Foolish Humpty-Dumpty! How silly you are for trusting me.' (sinister laughter) 'I'm the evil enemy, the arch criminal, the destroyer and the deceiver – Silly Humpty-Dumpty – Stupid Humpty-Dumpty – Gullible Humpty-Dumpty – Ruined Humpty-Dumpty – Dead Humpty-Dumpty. You've become a "scrambled egg" and your golden yolk is splashed across a thousand flowers in the King's country.' (sinister laughter) 'All the King's horses and all the King's men will never put you back together again.'

# 46
# Superstar

'Messiahmania', that's what they called it. Oh yeah! Who am I? I'm just a grass roots Rock journalist with the Melody Maker. I was given the job of following him around and covering all his Gigs. Oh, sorry, I didn't mention who I was following around: Jessie Richmaker, the most gifted and intelligent Rock musician of our time. The mystique of the man was phenomenal. It just knocked you out. Yeah sure, Hendrix had mystique, Dean had mystique, Joplin had mystique; some of the living heroes have mystique, Page, Dylan, Mercury, Springsteen, Jagger and Marley, a certain indefinable, almost legendary quality, but Jessie, man, he was out of this world; he was just beautiful.

Nobody knew exactly where he came from; that was the funhy part about the man. He seemed to be the child of a thousand cities and a thousand scowling nights, always on the move, always letting his music tell the truth. When pressed about his background, he referred ambiguously to a recording studio that nobody had ever heard of. What on earth did he call it? Oh yeah! I remember. He called the place 'Harmony House'. He never let on about its exact location. That was a guarded secret.

Jessie just turned up one day. Yeah! He just ambled casually into the Columbia recording studio like he owned the place, like he'd been expected for a thousand years. Nobody to this day knows exactly how he managed to get in. The place was guarded like a prison against the unwanted attention of hysterical fans.

If he hadn't been so good, the security guards would've been sacked on the spot and the alsatians sold to old ladies. He was tall, without being too tall; well built with a mop of blonde curls that were reminiscent of Frampton's hanging round his face like a flaming halo, but Jessie didn't look like a mediaeval saint. He was too dynamic, too contemporary. His chin was angular and strong, his lips were well formed and sensitive and his eyes, man, you should have seen them; they were a deep, inscrutable blue. You couldn't ask him any trick questions. He would just shoot you to bits with his eyes even before he spoke. Now look here, I've been interviewing superstars for about twelve years; I've talked to all the 'greats' of the sixties and the seventies, but man Jessie was the greatest. He just walked into the studio on that June morning with his Gibson guitar tucked like a lady under his arm, yeah, and knocked us all flat. After only a couple of songs, we were crawling round his feet like he was the Messiah, pleading for more. Yeah, I know! Hendrix was good. He was years ahead of his time, but Jessie was a million times better. There was no comparison. He just sat down on a vacant stool, took his sweet singing lady from her bed, tuned her up and began to sing and play. There was something about his style. He could make his guitar laugh, cry, scream with rage, whisper and sing. He could translate music. He was a unique talent; the kind of guy who turns up every thousand years or so, composes, plays, sings and then dies leaving a legend behind him. You could place him with Bach or Beethoven and he wouldn't look out of place. Mark my words – they're going to have a marble bust of Jessie adorning every archive of art on this little planet in another hundred years.

Look! I'm not biased. I'm a hardened Rock journalist. I've got over the adolescent idol stage, but man, the facts are there; millions felt it; that's why they screamed out 'Messiah' every time he walked on stage. Yeah, granted the music scene was at an all-time low. The 'gods' had gone to 'Desolation Row'. But Jessie took on the best of the old order and easily surpassed them. In fact, if the truth's known, that's why the other musicians didn't like him. He made them look like amateurs. He showed them up.

Sure, Jessie was strange. Some of the most gifted musicians in the world wanted the opportunity to play with him. He could give them status and a millionaire's life style. Jessie didn't want to know. He went out of his way to choose twelve unknown musicians. Maybe the title 'musician' would be a little too complimentary for the riff-raff that he picked up, but man, within a year his influence, his charisma, his sense of direction and purpose, his intelligent guidance and instruction, turned those twelve 'impossibles' into superlative musicians, some of the finest in the world.

Jessie could cope with the problems of superstardom like no other. Dylan collapsed, Clapton collapsed, Lennon collapsed, but Jessie was a 'natural'; he could cope easily. It was like he was born to be a Superstar. He would sit and sign autograph books and talk to the kids for hours after a concert. He felt responsible for them. He didn't want to exploit them. He wanted to show them the way. It was during one of his long conversations with his fans that he first mentioned 'Harmony House'. 'That's the place where I come from', he said, 'and I wish this old earth could be a "Harmony House".' It was like the Woodstock dream again, but better, more real.

It was Jessie's unpopularity with the other Rock Superstars that finally precipitated his downfall. They didn't realise that the place where a shooting star falls, often becomes a centre for pilgrimage. Jessie was a shooting star, an omen of hope to a generation. The other Rock Superstars were jealous, green all over. Everywhere they looked they saw him. His face was constantly seen on television; his well-known profile was slashed across every newspaper and magazine in the country, the 'Messiah of Rock'. Yeah, and that's when the outsiders became collaborators. It was the biggest sell-out ever. They, the Rock Elite, told the Authorities, the High Priests of the System, that Jessie was dangerous. Jessie dangerous! Man, you must be joking. He was the holiest in all the land. He never dreamt of leading a violent revolution. He was no 'Street Fighting Man'. He just wanted to make music and obviate discord. I can see him now, standing with his guitar by a caravan of lorries loaded with equipment. All he ever wanted to do was to promote harmony, not to introduce a reign of terror. He didn't want to see his fans, his loyal fans, lying naked in the streets and gutters like so many broken dolls, shot to bits by the Army and Police. That just wasn't his way. The Government was concerned. They had no innate distrust of any idol who could sing and play guitar and capture the beleaguered imagination of a generation, and anyway, all this talk about love, peace and harmony was unnatural. It reminded them of the San Francisco thing: the flowers, the free love, the 'grass' and 'acid'! The Police were out to put him down. They bugged his hotel rooms, sent him threatening letters and began a propaganda campaign to smash his reputation. It worked. Overnight, Jessie became another Timothy Leary, another Ken Kesy, another Charles Manson. He became the true 'Outsider', the lonely outlaw hunted by the Establishment, and the kids loved him more for it. They held him to their heart. They all knew that their 'Messiah' was going to be taken. Society had put him on a death trip and he was nearing the end of his journey.

When it finally happened, no one was surprised, it was anticipated. One of his musicians, a friend at that, betrayed him. He was shot. They didn't make a mistake. His car was riddled with bullet holes and so was his guitar and guitar case. His blood stretched out across the nation like highways on a map. But they had forgotten one thing: You can kill a man but you can't kill his music; when you kill a man, you make a legend, 'Messiahmania' was just beginning. 'Jessie still alive!' read the newspapers, and from a million tongues across the nations, a generation emerging from betrayal and uncertainty, came the reply: 'Jessie still lives!'

All the High Priests of the System will be forgotten. Some will be relegated to the pages of history books to spend eternity in enforced retirement. All the so called Superstars will leave the stage of memory in disgrace, but Jessie, man, he'll live forever. They'll be singing his songs in a thousand years, and one day, this old earth will be a 'Harmony House', just like Jessie said.

# 47
# The Dance Master

NARRATOR:   In the beginning was the Dance Master,
Dancing among the star flowers
In the meadows of space.
And he said: 'I will make a soul.'
And he made a soul and taught her the steps of his dance,
And he gave her a baby
  Who became a child,
    Who became a man.
In his youth he learnt the steps of the dance;
The soul was his teacher
And they were happy together.

The soul became beautiful.
In the dance she grew in loveliness
Until another dancer appeared,
  And another,
    And another.
WEALTH:
My name is Wealth. I will teach you the steps of my
dance and you will be richer than a king.
FAME:
My name is Fame. I will teach you the steps of my
dance and you will be greater than a king.
AMBITION:
My name is Ambition. I will teach you the steps of my
dance and you will be stronger than a king.
NARRATOR:
The Dance of the Dance Master are forgotten.
We will dance the steps of the world, you and I,
And grow rich together.
SOUL:
Why have you stopped dancing the steps that I was
taught by the Dance Master?
MAN:
Silence! The steps of the Dance Master are forgotten.

We will dance the steps of the world, you and I,
And grow rich together.

NARRATOR:
The soul obeyed
But her loveliness withered
Like the petals of a flower.
She grew old before her time
And her limbs forgot the music of the dance.
At last the man called her to his presence.

MAN:
Soul! Soul! The time has come for me to retire.
We will dance the dance of the world
On the mosaic floor
Beneath the artificial sunlight
Of a thousand crystal chandeliers,
And 'live, drink and be merry'.

SOUL:
I will dance with you.
I have forgotten the steps
That the Dance Master taught me
In the days of my innocence.
You have taught me the steps of your dance . . .
The dance of the world.

NARRATOR:
And so they danced the dances
Of Wealth, Fame and Ambition,
But their dancing was confused and ugly.

*THE ARRIVAL OF THE DANCE MASTER.*

DANCE MASTER:
You fool! Today your soul is required of you.
You have neglected my dance and have danced
The steps of the world. Come! (The soul departs)

MAN:
Come back!

DANCE MASTER:
Fool! (The man dies)

# 48
# The Football

Sammy was a football, a beautiful brown leather football. He was purchased at an exhorbitant price from 'Bouncing Balls' for the Wembley Cup Final. I anticipate your question: 'which Cup Final?' Let me think. It was the famous Cup Final of '71', 1971; Bristol City versus the favourites West Ham. Sammy had the privilege of being the football of the match. Quite an honour, don't you think?

The great day arrived; armies of chanting fans in their uniforms of coloured rosettes and scarves descended on the Stadium from a thousand different directions. When at last Sammy was placed on the centre spot between the two opposing sides, he felt most unhappy. Like most brilliantly gifted footballs, he was rather temperamental and unnecessarily bouncy. When he was carried on the field in the arms of the referee, nobody noticed him. They were too busy applauding their respective teams to acknowledge the debut of Sammy the football. This, I am sorry to say, hurt poor Sammy deeply. 'Nobody loves me', he mumbled in self-pity. The referee's whistle blew shrilly and the West Ham captain was just about to kick off, when Sammy, feeling positively rebellious, complained bitterly. He just couldn't stand being kicked around. 'If you kick me, I'm going to notify my Union'. The captain eyed the offending football in sheer disbelief. Having recovered sufficiently from the shock, he again prepared to kick Sammy. The tension of the match, he thought, had affected the balance of his mind. Who's ever heard of a football talking! As the captain lifted up his right foot in preparation to kick, Sammy barked an abrupt command: 'Stop!' The captain nearly jumped out of his football boots and socks. 'If you kick me', continued the angry football, 'I'm going to notify my Union and we'll call a general strike.' By this time, the crowd had begun to whistle and cheer threateningly. Never had a captain in the history of English football, behaved in such an eccentric manner.

From a distance it appeared as if he was doing a war dance in front of what seemed to be a very innocuous football. Unfortunately, the Bristol City players were under the impression that the captain's behaviour was some kind of clever psychological trick. Their captain, who was becoming angry at the delay, shouted: 'Stop dancing and stop doing that stupid ventriloquist act and get on with the game.' In spite of Sammy's passionate protests, the West Ham captain had no alternative. Cursing his misfortune, he summoned up every ounce of courage and kicked Sammy fiercely in the stomach, sending him spinning rapidly into the Bristol City half of the field. You might find this hard to believe, but that little incident cost West Ham the game. Sammy had it in for them. Every time they had a free kick or an open shot at the goal, he would purposely bounce away from the white posts.

During the last quarter of the second half, Sammy complained bitterly to the referee. 'Hey mate', he said, 'I don't like being kicked about and knocked from one end of the field to another. I was born for better things than a dizzy head and bruised body.' The referee blew his whistle and brought the game to an abrupt halt. He then ran quickly to Sammy, picked him cautiously up, shook him vigorously to see if he rattled, bounced him a couple of times and then looked at him very carefully. The impatient crowd began to hiss and cheer. There was only one thing for it. He slowly put his hand into his pocket and pulled out his little book with the intention of taking Sammy's name. Sammy was livid with rage. 'Your head would you like to be kicked around,' said the furious football. 'How would make a wonderful football. It's big and ugly enough.' The referee blushed bright crimson. He blew his whistle fiercely and brandished the yellow card like a loaded revolver.

'Get off this pitch, you insolent football,' he screamed. Sammy rolled happily from the field singing that famous Liverpool classic, 'You'll never roll alone'. He was the centre of attention at last!

Both managers gave Sammy a good 'kicking off'. Eventually it was decided he should go and see a well-known psychiatrist. Unwillingly he complied, and after a long and embarrassing period of interrogation, he was told in no uncertain language that he needed love. His anti-social behaviour had been precipitated by exploitation. He felt that people were kicking him about without caring for him. If only the crowd had cheered when he was carried into the Stadium; if only the players had kissed him and patted him lovingly after he had bounded into the goal net, things would have been so different. The psychiatrist said that he needed individual significance. 'What you need,' he said as Sammy was about to depart, 'is identity and love.' It had become obvious during the interview that he was terribly afraid of becoming old and shabby; he rolled in horror from the day when he would be torn, dirty wrinkled and the air would leave his rubber lung in a protracted gasp, and he, Sammy the football, would be thrown into an FA dustbin. He desperately needed someone who would buy him for what he was, someone who would polish him regularly and show him a great deal of love and concern. Unfortunately for Sammy, he was never purchased by such a person, and eventually, crowded stadiums with a hundred thousand screaming fans, rotating television cameras and skilful feet with iron toe caps that sent one spinning across a battlefield of green turf, gave way to a lonely FA dustbin, to end his short life in the desolation of ten thousand empty stands, amongst the debris and the rubbish of the hordes of fans.

# 49
# The incomparable Christ

'More than nineteen hundred years ago, there was a man born contrary to the laws of life.
This man lived in poverty and was reared in obscurity. He did not travel extensively; only once did he cross the boundary of the country in which he lived.
He possessed neither wealth nor influence;
His relatives were inconspicuous and uninfluential, and had neither training nor education.

In infancy, he startled a king; in childhood, he puzzled doctors; in manhood, he ruled the course of nature, walking upon billows as if they were pavements, and hushing the sea to sleep.
He healed the multitudes without medicine, and made no charge for his services.

He never wrote a book – yet all the libraries of the country could not hold the books that have been written about him.
He never wrote a song – but he has furnished the theme for more songs than all the songwriters combined.
He never founded a college – yet all the schools put together cannot boast of having as many students.
He never practiced medicine – yet he has healed more broken hearts than all the doctors far and near.

He never marshalled an army, drafted a soldier, nor fired a gun, yet no leader has ever had more volunteers who, under his orders have made more rebels stack arms and surrender without firing a shot.

Every seventh day, the wheels of commerce cease their turning and multitudes wind their way, as worshipping assemblers pay homage and respect to him.
The names of the past proud statesmen of Greece and Rome have come and gone, but the name of this man abounds more and more.

Although time has spread nineteen hundred years between the people of this generation and the scene of his crucifixion, he still lives.
Herod could not kill him, Satan could not seduce him, death could not destroy him, and the grave could not hold him,
He stands forth upon the highest pinnacle of heavenly glory – proclaimed of God, acknowledged by angels, adored by saints, feared by devils – as the living, personal Christ, our Lord and Saviour!'

# 50
# The long silence

At the end of time billions of people were scattered on a great
plain before God's throne.
Most shrank from the brilliant light before them,
But some groups near the front talked heatedly – not with
cringing shame but with belligerence.

'Can God judge us? How can he know about suffering?' snapped
a pert young brunette. She ripped open a sleeve to reveal a
tattooed number from a Nazi concentration camp.
'We endured terror, beatings, torture, death.'

In another group a Negro boy lowered his collar.
'What about this?' he demanded, showing an ugly rope burn:
'Lynched for no other crime than being black!'

In another crowd a pregnant schoolgirl with sullen eyes.
'Why should I suffer?' she murmured. 'It wasn't my fault.'
Far out across the plain were hundreds of such groups.
Each had a complaint against God for the evil and suffering
He permitted in this world.
'How lucky God was to live in heaven where all the sweetness and
light, where there was no weeping or fear, no hunger or hatred!
What did God know of all that men had been forced to endure in
this world? For God leads a pretty sheltered life,' they said.

So each of these groups sent forth their leader, chosen because he
had suffered most. A Jew, a Negro, a person from Hiroshima, a
horribly deformed arthritic and a thalidomide child.
In the centre of the plain they consulted with each other.
At last they were ready to present their case. It was rather clever.

Before God could be qualified to be their judge, he must endure what
they had endured. Their decision was that God should be sentenced
to live on earth – as a man.

Let him be born a Jew. Let the legitimacy of his birth be doubted.
Give him a work so difficult so that even his family will think him
out of his mind when he tries to do it. Let him be betrayed by
his closest friends. Let him face false charges, Be tried by a
prejudice judge. Let him be tortured.

At last let him see what it means to be terribly alone. Then let
him die. Let him die so that there can be no doubt that he died.
Let there be a whole host of witnesses to verify it.
As each leader announced his portion of the sentence loud murmurs
of approval went up from the throng of people assembled.

When the last had finished pronouncing sentence there was a
long silence.
No one uttered another word. No one moved.
For suddenly all knew that
God had already served his sentence.

If you wish to receive *regular information* about *new books,* please send your name and address to:

London Bible Warehouse
PO Box 123
Basingstoke
Hants RG23 7NL

Name _____

Address _____

_____

_____

_____

I am especially interested in:
- ☐ Biographies
- ☐ Fiction
- ☐ Christian living
- ☐ Issue related books
- ☐ Academic books
- ☐ Bible study aids
- ☐ Children's books
- ☐ Music
- ☐ Other subjects

P.S. If you have ideas for new Christian Books or other products, please write to us too!

## Other Marshall Pickering Paperbacks

## LOVING GOD

*Charles Colson*

Loving God is the very purpose of the believer's life, the vocation for which he is made. However loving God is not easy and most people have given little real thought to what the greatest commandment really means.

Many books have been written on the individual subjects of repentence, Bible study, prayer, outreach, evangelism, holiness and other elements of the Christian life. In **Loving God**, Charles Colson draws all these elements together to look at the entire process of growing up as a Christian.

Combining vivid illustrations with straightforward exposition he shows how to live out the Christian faith in our daily lives. **Loving God** provides a real challenge to deeper commitment and points the way towards greater maturity.

## THROUGH DAVID'S PSALMS

*Derek Prince*

Derek Prince, internationally known Bible teacher and scholar, draws on his understanding of the Hebrew language and culture, and a comprehensive knowledge of Scripture, to present 101 meditations from the Psalms.

Each of these practical and enriching meditations is based on a specific passage and concludes with a faith response. They can be used either for personal meditation or for family devotions. They are intended for all those who want their lives enriched or who seek comfort and encouragement from the Scriptures.

# DREADLOCKS

*Les Isaacs*

Les Isaacs knew what it was to hate. He was brought up to believe in England as the land of milk and honey. However, when his parents came here in 1965, he found as a young boy that the cramped basement flats of Islington and the racial prejudice he encountered at school did not match up to the promise. Being tough and independent he became an adept street fighter and by the age of thirteen was leading West Indian gangs in running street battles with white skinheads. The collapse of one dream led him to explore others and in his teens he identified fully with Rastafarian way of life, with its stylish dreadlocks, heavy ganja smoking and vision of liberation from white political and economic slavery. But the inner peace and freedom he sought was not there. Indeed his life was in turmoil.

After a family row he was on the verge of killing his father when he heard a clear proclamation of the Gospel that transformed his life.

The change was complete and the desire to witness to his former friends, other Rastafarians, and young blacks has led him into full-time evangelism in London's deprived inner city areas.


# RELEASE
## The Miracle of the Siberian Seven

*Timothy Chmykhalov with Danny Smith*

The plight of the 'Siberian Seven' attracted widespread publicity and support.

Timothy Chmykhalov, youngest member of the seven, vividly recounts the events leading to the entry into the US Embassy in 1978, the long years of hoping and waiting, the uncertainty which faced them when they left in 1983 and finally the freedom which they found in America.

**Release** is a powerful testimony of faith and courage amidst intense pressure and threat of persecution. A story of hope and determination in the face of much discouragement.

# RACE FOR LIFE

*Janet Sonnenberg*

On September 15, 1979 Joel, his sister Jami and their parents Mike and Janet were involved in a terrible car accident. Twenty-two month old Joel was trapped in his infant seat in a blazing inferno of twisted metal. Miraculously he survived, albeit with horrific burns over most of his body.

**Race for Life** is the remarkable account of this child's undaunted spirit and courage. It is the dramatic story of the power of God in the lives of Mike and Janet as they experienced His daily presence, promises and provisions in the midst of circumstances that would normally have meant complete devastation. It is also a powerful testimony to the love of the Christian community as they responded to the desperate need of this little boy and his family.

Once you have met Joel Sonnenberg, in the pages of this book, you will never forget him or his parents. You will gain spiritual perspective and dimension for your own life as you read about this family's struggle to survive indescribable pain and suffering, both as individuals and as a unit, and as they seek God's healing redirection in their lives.

# OUT OF THE MELTING POT

*Bob Gordon*

Faith does not operate in a vacuum, it operates in human lives. God wants your life to be a crucible of faith.

Bob Gordon draws together Biblical principles and personal experience to provide valuable insights into this key area. Particular reference is made to the lessons he leant recently as God provided £600,000 to buy Roffey Place Christian Training Centre.

**Out of the Melting Pot** is Bob Gordon's powerful testimony to the work of God today and a profound challenge to shallow views of faith.